From
THE
Heart

From
THE
Heart

*Bible Stories for
Today's Woman*

CAROLYN LARSEN

HENDRICKSON
PUBLISHERS

From the Heart: Bible Stories for Today's Woman

Copyright © 2001 by Carolyn Larsen
Published by Hendrickson Publishers
P.O. Box 3473
Peabody, Massachusetts, 01961-3473

Printed in the United States of America

ISBN 1-56563-650-3

First printing—June 2001

Cover design by Richmond & Williams, Nashville, Tennessee
Interior design and typesetting by Reider Publishing Services,
    San Francisco, California
Edited by Judy Bodmer, Gwen Waller, and Deneen Sedlack

Table of Contents

Acknowledgments

WRITING A BOOK CAN BE A LONELY and sometimes overwhelming project. There were many days when I wondered why I thought I could possibly do this. God surrounded me with many people who offered encouragement, help, and prayer support along the way. Please allow me to say a brief thank you to those people:

To the wonderful folks at Hendrickson Publishers, especially Dan Penwell—thanks for the opportunity, encouragement, and patience.

To Judy Bodmer, Gwen Waller, and Deneen Sedlack—thank you for your superb editing, proofreading, and attention to detail. Your care and acumen gave my writing added clarity and character.

To my Bible study friends, Barbara, Karen, Miffy, and Vicki— your insights into Scripture have enriched me and your personal walks with God have inspired me.

To my husband, Eric, and children, Cori, Mallory, and Ryan. Thanks for putting up with a cloistered mom, for eating frozen pizza, doing your own laundry, and through it all, offering constant "you-can-do-it" cheers.

My heartfelt gratitude to each of you.

Introduction

REMEMBER THE BIBLE STORY OF THE woman who was sick for twelve years? In a moment of total faith, she reached through a crowd of people and brushed her fingers against the hem of Jesus' robe. This, she believed, would make her well . . . and indeed, it did.

Not long ago a friend and I were discussing this story. As we talked, the reality of what this woman of faith may have experienced truly grabbed my heart. It was then that I realized how accustomed, yes, even numb I had become to the stories of the Bible.

Most of us know the Bible stories that are retold in From the Heart. We may have heard them for years, taught them in Sunday school, or studied them in Bible classes. But . . . there is a danger in this familiarity. When stories are so well known, our minds tend to skip over the experiences and lesson to be learned from these characters.

From the Heart is not a how-to-be-a-better-Christian-in-five-easy-steps book. It is more about an opportunity to rethink the experiences of these Bible characters from a modern, personal point of view and then, reflect on their failures, on their victories, and on the way God interacted with them and constantly loved them.

None of us have achieved the ultimate in our relationship with God. Knowing him is a journey . . . a process. My hope is that reading these Bible stories, and reflecting on their meaning will move you into deeper intimacy with our gracious, loving God.

Paying the Piper

"PSSSST, HEY, LADY! OVER HERE!"

Eve looked around, but didn't see anyone except Adam, and he was busy down at the river. So who had called her? Shrugging, she took a bite of the sweet, ripe fruit. Juice trickled down her arm. Sensing that someone was watching her, Eve looked up. Before her was the most beautiful creature she'd ever seen. "I know all the animals in the garden . . . but I've never seen you before." She circled it admiringly and asked, "Who are you?"

"It's not important," he hissed. "Why are you eating *that*? You could be enjoying the sweetest fruit in the garden."

"What do you mean?" she asked.

"I know a fruit that is much sweeter than anything you've ever tasted."

The serpent gently drew Eve toward the tree in the center of the garden. Eve dismissed the idea with a wave of her hand. "God said to stay away from that tree. He said we will die if we even touch it."

"Oh, come on. God won't kill you for touching a tree. The fruit on that tree will make you more like God. Try it," he whispered.

Eve was confused. The fruit was shiny and it looked juicy. Impulsively she grabbed one and took a bite. The flavor was incredible.

"Adam, taste this. It's absolutely heavenly!" Eve shoved the fruit into her husband's hand.

When Adam saw what it was, he was terrified. "Don't you remember what God said?" Eve waved the fruit in his face. It smelled sweet, and the thick yellow juice ran between her fingers and dripped onto his toes.

"Oh, Adam, I tasted it and I didn't die. The serpent said God wouldn't kill us. Just taste it." Adam wanted to resist. After all, God had given them only one rule. But he couldn't take his eyes off that fruit, and Eve did seem to be okay. Adam leaned forward and took a bite. Instantly, he knew nothing would ever be the same.

Later, God came to the garden and discovered Adam and Eve hiding from him. He knew what had happened. Adam passed the blame to Eve: "She gave me the fruit!" Eve passed it right to the serpent: "He tricked me!" God knew what had happened. He didn't hide his disappointment. "I have to punish you, but that doesn't mean I don't love you. I'll always love you—no matter what."

BASED ON GENESIS 3

 Reflections From The Heart

"But, officer, I had to speed to stay with the flow of traffic." "I lost my temper only because you were being such a putz." "Why do you always have to do that?" How many times have I tried to justify my sin by blaming someone else? Why do I do my best to avoid punishment, even if I actually deserve it? Because it might be painful? Because I want to avoid the embarrassment of anyone knowing I've messed up? Or maybe, deep down, I'm afraid that my repeated failures might cause God to stop loving me. Probably all these reasons, and others have motivated me at various times. The bottom line is, I'm proud, and I don't want to admit failure.

Yet, admitting sin is basic to my faith. I must acknowledge, to myself and to God that I mess up every day. Oh sure, I may not commit murder, or abuse a child, or rob a bank. My sins are much more subtle; some are even socially acceptable. But, when I stand before God with all the social trimmings stripped away, sin is sin. The fact of the matter is, in my heart I know when I've sinned, so who do I think I'm kidding?

God knew I would sin daily, if not in my actions, then certainly in my attitudes, and he has already handled the situation. Jesus was nailed to a cross for my sins. Every clank of the hammer was a cleansing stroke for me. Because I am a Christian, his death covers my sins—they are already forgiven.

So, what can I learn from Adam and Eve? They messed up, disobeying the one rule God had given them. Then, they tried to hide from him, cover up their sin, and pass the blame. But they didn't fool God. He knew what they had done and who was responsible. He had to punish them. But—and this is important—he didn't stop loving them. Their relationship with him didn't end that day in the garden. So, I learn to admit my sins and ask for his forgiveness. Then, I believe that he forgives and that his love never stops flowing.

The challenge for today: When you mess up, confess, accept the punishment, learn from the experience, and move on, because God does.

"Therefore, since we have been justified through faith, we have peace with God through our Lord Jesus Christ." —ROMANS 5:1

Telltale Heart

CAIN HAD A CHIP ON HIS SHOULDER THE size of Egypt. He seemed to resent his younger brother more every day, complaining that Abel didn't work hard enough or do his share of chores. Ever since they were little boys, Cain had whined that Abel didn't play fair, and he had picked on Abel instead of teaching and protecting him. He even made fun of Abel's job, "Hey, shepherd boy, why don't you get a real job? All you do is follow stupid sheep around all day. How hard is that?" Cain went back to working in his field, snickering and sneering at his brother.

One afternoon Cain was checking his fence line when he noticed Abel building a stone altar. He stopped and watched his brother put an offering on the altar, then kneel to worship God. *That's one of his prize lambs. What kind of fool sacrifices his best lamb? Well, if he's giving an offering to God, I guess I have to give one, too,* Cain thought. *But I'm no fool. I'm not cutting down my best grain. I'll just use some of the scraggly stuff from the edges of the field. No one will know anyway.* So, Cain quickly made his offering, but to his surprise, God refused it.

"Hey! You accepted Abel's offering. What's wrong with mine? That creep Abel is always everybody's favorite! It's not fair!" Cain was so angry that he stomped across the field, unaware that he was crushing the very grain that he had felt was too good to give to God.

"Watch your heart, Cain. If you sacrifice with the right attitude, I'll accept it, too," God told him.

But, Cain was never one to be concerned with his attitude; he couldn't admit that he was wrong. He decided to take matters into his own hands. "Abel my bro', I know I've been hard on you lately, and I want you to know that I'm sorry. Look, I need some help out in my field; could you lend a hand?" Abel was happy to help his brother. But, when they got to the field, Cain picked up a rock and bashed Abel in the head. Abel fell down, dead. "So much for my holier-than-thou brother," Cain sneered.

Later that day he was quite surprised when God asked, "Where's Abel?"

"How should I know? It's not my day to watch him!" Cain snapped. Then God told him that Abel's blood was crying out from the ground. God knew that Cain had murdered his brother. Not only did God refuse Cain's offering, now he would punish Cain, too.

BASED ON GENESIS 4:1–16

 Reflections From The Heart

Cain, Cain, Cain. Who did he think he was fooling? Have you ever known anyone who always seemed to have a chip on his shoulder? That kind of person is not much fun to be around. The crazy thing is, Cain was jealous because Abel was a nice guy who had his life straight with God. Cain could have enjoyed the same relationship with God, but he was too lazy or selfish. So, instead of actually doing business with God and getting straight with him, Cain tried to fake it. Fool. To rephrase an old expression, "You can fool some of the people some of the time, but you can't ever fool God." God gave Cain the key when he told him, "Watch your heart," but Cain paid no attention.

Yeah, it's easy to criticize Cain; he really messed up. But, to learn from him, we have to get personal. Have you ever gone to church or Bible study and said the right words, sang the praise choruses, quoted Bible verses, and prayed the eloquent prayers, when all the time your heart was angry at your husband? Have you ever smiled and said the appropriate kind words to a friend, when in your heart you were jealous of her lovely home or her creativity? Well, who do you think you're fooling? God knows what's going on in your heart. All the fancy finery on the outside is not fooling him one bit.

The challenge for today: Guard your heart. When something is wrong between you and God or you and another person, get it straightened out before it does real damage.

"Above all else, guard your heart, for it is the wellspring of life."
—PROVERBS 4:23

Yes, Dear . . .

"HONEY, I'M GOING TO BUILD A BOAT," announced Noah. S-i-l-e-n-c-e. "Did you hear me? I've got to run to the lumber yard to pick up some materials . . . cypress wood, pitch, buckets, brushes . . . let's see, what else will I need? Honey, what are you doin'?"

S-i-l-e-n-c-e. Noah wandered through the house, looking for his wife. He found her washing dishes, sort of. Actually, the plate that she had been holding was lying shattered on the floor. "Oops, you dropped a plate." Noah swept up the pieces as he babbled about the boat. It took a few minutes before he realized that his wife was not responding. He finally asked, "What's the matter?"

"You're going to build a . . . boat? Why? What about your job? How are we going to pay for the supplies?" Questions tumbled from Noah's wife faster than she could spit them out. With each one her voice grew louder and shriller until she shouted, "Why are you building a boat?"

"God told me to," Noah said quietly.

S-i-l-e-n-c-e. "Ummm, well, uh, why didn't you, ah, say so?"

Noah quietly explained, "God is fed up with the way people are behaving. You know how evil and wicked the world has become. People think only of themselves and have no regard for God at all. He's tired of it. So, he's sending a big flood—it will cover the whole earth. Because our family honors him, he warned me about it and even told me exactly how to build the boat . . . a very big boat. We'll survive; then he wants us to repopulate the earth after the flood."

"So, a flood, huh? Well, if God says to build a boat, then you'd better build a boat. I'll help you however I can. You'd better get busy."

"Yes, I'd better. Oh, uhh, one more thing. It's a little thing really, hardly even worth mentioning. God is going to send a few animals to go on the boat with us."

"Animals? Like rabbits and birds?"

"Yes, those and, oh, you know, snakes, tigers, uhhh, spiders."

"Spiders? Do there have to be spiders?" S-i-l-e-n-c-e. "Well, (gulp) whatever God says."

BASED ON GENESIS 6:1–7:9

 Reflections From The Heart

Mrs. Noah doesn't get much press in most accounts of the Great Flood, but she must have been a go-with-the-flow kind of woman. Even in her culture, where wives could not give much input, Noah's decision had big implications for her, too. Everything in their family must have changed when Noah began to devote time to building the ark. Plus, their friends and neighbors may have wondered if Noah had a screw loose and they probably distanced themselves from the Noahs. So, other than the stress of building the ark, it more than likely was a lonely time for the family.

Going with the flow meant Noah's wife had to give up her own agenda. For example, what if she had planned to buy wallpaper for the kitchen with the money Noah was using for building supplies? What if she wanted him to spend his time helping her put in an herb garden? For the whole ark thing to work, Mrs. Noah had to let go of her own agenda and trust Noah. Otherwise she would have had to learn to tread water.

What can we learn from the lady of the Noah household? Don't hate me, but the word submission has to come up. Mrs. Noah supported her husband in obeying God, even though she didn't hear God's command, and even though it may have been socially unpleasant and inconvenient. She trusted her husband's relationship with God and submitted to the command God gave him.

OK, true confession—I'm not very good at submission, even though I know that scripturally God has placed my husband as the head of our home. It's not because I don't trust him or I don't love him. It's because I sometimes have trouble letting go of my agenda. Of course, at times I'm good at going with the flow—when it's my idea.

How are you at going with the flow? Do you give God room to guide someone else? Do you trust that person enough to work side by side with him or her? Remember, a lot more can be accomplished by two working together than by one working here and another working there.

The challenge for today: Ask yourself if you need to lighten up a little, be a little less rigid, a little more trusting. Don't think so? Well, maybe you can swim better than I can.

"Two are better than one, because they have a good return for their work: If one falls down, his friend can help him up. But pity the man who falls and has no one to help him up!" —ECCLESIASTES 4:9–10

Liver Spots and Stretch Marks

S ARAH'S OLD BACK ACHED AND HER varicose-veined legs were weak. *Cooking when it's this hot ought to be against the law,* she thought. *Oh well, at least Abraham and those three men seem to be enjoying dinner.* She leaned against the tent door to rest for a minute when a bit of the men's conversation caught her ear. "Baby . . . this time next year . . . ." Sarah leaned farther out the door and listened closely. "Sarah will have a baby by this time next year."

"A baby? That man thinks I'm going to have a baby?" The idea struck Sarah so funny that a giggle formed deep in her belly and bubbled up through her body until it shot right out her mouth. She had to hold on to the doorframe to keep from collapsing with laughter. "God promised us a baby years ago, but look at me. I'm old and wrinkled, and my body is drying up. If I had a baby now, I'd look like his grandmother, not his mother!"

"Why is your wife laughing?" asked one of the men. "Doesn't she believe God can give you a baby?" Poor Abraham didn't know what to say. Sarah clamped her hand over her mouth to stop the laughter.

A few months later, when she was battling morning sickness, swollen ankles, and strange food cravings, Sarah knew the idea wasn't so preposterous. About a year later, Sarah and Abraham cuddled their baby boy, Isaac, and thanked God for keeping his wonderful promise.

BASED ON GENESIS 18:1–15; 21:1–7

 Reflections From The Heart

Yeah, who would think that God could do the impossible? After all, that would mean that God controls the universe and has power over all nature. Yet, God had made an audible promise to Abraham and Sarah: "Look up at the heavens and count the stars—if indeed you can count them. . . . So shall your offspring be" (Genesis 15:5). Would the God of the universe keep his promise? Even if it was years and years later?

Yes! Sarah should have known that, even though the prospect of her wrinkled body birthing a baby seemed totally impossible. The God who created the world, then recreated it after the Great Flood could do whatever he said he would do.

This story has real implications for our prayer lives, doesn't it? Do we truly believe that we can trust God's character? Can we trust him to do what he says he will do? Or, do we sometimes make our own definition of God and decide that he can do this . . . but he can't do that. I wonder what blessings we miss because we simply don't believe?

The challenge for today: Believe what God says in his Word. Trust him to do the seemingly impossible. Then, enjoy what he does!

"God, who has called you into fellowship with his Son Jesus Christ our Lord, is faithful." —1 CORINTHIANS 1:9

God First

"MAMA, I'M GOING WITH DADDY TO make a sacrifice to God!" Isaac called as he danced around Sarah.

"Stand still, Isaac, I can't make heads or tails of what you're saying. Dad is going to let you go with him to the mountain?" For some reason, a hint of fear rolled through Sarah's heart. She looked at Abraham with questioning eyes, but he wouldn't meet her gaze.

"Go pack, Son." Abraham's voice sounded strange. "We'll leave early tomorrow." Isaac skipped away, too excited to sleep. "Isn't he a little young?" Sarah asked softly.

Abraham was quiet for a moment before answering, "Isaac is a gift from God—the fulfillment of a promise. We must trust God and believe that he loves us . . . and Isaac." Sarah wondered what his odd statement meant, but she was afraid to ask more.

The next morning, Isaac ran ahead of Abraham as they left for the mountain. Sarah was still uneasy, but not sure why. Then it hit her. Abraham always took along a lamb to sacrifice. Today he carried the fire, but no lamb. "O God, what's going on? You wouldn't ask that, would you? You wouldn't ask for our precious son! God, you gave him to us . . . ." Sarah's breath caught in her throat as she realized what she had just said. "Yes, you gave him to us. He's yours. He's yours." Her voice trailed away into whispered sobs.

The next few days were the longest of Sarah's life. Finally she heard Isaac calling, "Mama! Guess what? I was going to be the sacrifice! Daddy tied me up and took out his big knife. Then God's angel yelled for him to stop, and he showed us a ram stuck in the bush and we sacrificed it and . . . it was cool!" Sarah caught Isaac in a hug so hard that he wiggled to get free. Through her tears she looked at her husband, who was crying, too.

BASED ON GENESIS 22:1–14

 ## Reflections From The Heart

Thankfully, our loving Father probably will never ask us to make a choice as harsh as Abraham had to make. But the fact is, our God is a jealous God. He doesn't want to share our worship and devotion with anyone or anything. In the Old Testament, we repeatedly read of God's displeasure when the people turned away from him and looked to false gods. He found some creative means of getting their attention again.

By outward appearances, we can seem to be completely devoted to God, attending church, using our gifts, even reading the Bible and praying on a somewhat regular basis. But he looks beyond the external, right to the heart. That sometimes gets me into trouble because, no matter how devout I appear, my heart may be totally screwed up. For example, I really love my kids. Now, that doesn't make me any different from 99.9 percent of the world's moms. But, at times I focus totally on my children and what is happening in their lives, who is treating them unfairly, what struggles they are facing, and how I can help them. I focus more on them than I do on God. You know what I'm talking about, don't you? I even try to tell God how to help them. (After all, they're my kids, and who knows them better than I do?)

Of course, putting God in first place doesn't mean that I love my kids or my husband any less; I just love God more. Everything in life goes more smoothly when God holds his proper position in my heart, and I'm not trying to pull the wool over his eyes by my outside behavior.

The challenge for today: Make a conscious effort every day to keep God first, realizing that all of life will go better when he is on the throne in your heart.

"Love the LORD your God with all your heart and with all your soul and with all your strength." —DEUTERONOMY 6:5

Forgive? Forget It!

JOSEPH'S BROTHERS HATED HIM. THEIR dad so obviously favored him that he had even given Joseph a fancy coat like rich people wore. Did any of them get coats? Of course not. Then Joseph bragged to his brothers (well, to them it sounded like bragging) that he had dreamed they were bowing down to him. Yeah, right. Joseph's brothers came up with a plan to get rid of him. They tossed him into a dried up well. He yelled and whined to get out, but they ignored him. They didn't care if he died. Then one brother had an attack of conscience and came up with another idea. Noticing a caravan of men heading to Egypt, he suggested, "Let's sell Joseph to those guys on their way to Egypt. They can sell him to be a slave."

Next thing Joseph knew he was a slave in the house of Potiphar. The army officer was impressed with Joseph's honesty and hard work, and he put him in charge of the whole household. Things were looking good until Potiphar's wife got mad at Joseph and had him thrown in jail.

Even in jail he prayed every day, seeking God's help and guidance. "Hey kid, have you noticed that you're still in jail? Your prayers aren't working," the other prisoners taunted. But, when God helped Joseph explain Pharaoh's dreams, Pharaoh made Joseph second in command of the whole country. Not bad for a former slave boy!

In the dreams God warned that a food shortage was coming. Joseph came up with a food storage plan, which he managed for the next seven years. Then, when the nations around Egypt were starving, people came to Joseph to buy grain.

One day he looked out at the crowd of people waiting to purchase food, and he saw his brothers. Joseph could have tossed them into jail to pay them back for selling him into slavery. He could have had them killed on the spot—he certainly had the power to do that. But, what did Joseph do? He forgave them and brought them to live with him in Egypt.

BASED ON GENESIS 37–45

 Reflections From The Heart

Joseph was quite a guy, wasn't he? His brothers treated him like dirt, his life hit some rough spots, but he stayed true to God. He even prayed while he was in prison. Then, when the opportunity to get even with his brothers unexpectedly popped up, he didn't take it. He forgave them and went the extra mile by bringing them to live with him.

Medical experts tell us that if we hold a grudge, it only hurts us. The energy expended can actually make us physically ill. So, we don't get even with the person who hurt us; we just make ourselves sick. Our mental energy is focused on nursing that grudge. Even if we try to get involved in other things, our thoughts snap back to that grudge, just like a stretched out rubber band snaps back to its original size. Letting go of anger and hurt and then moving forward is much healthier.

Has someone hurt you? Have you been able to let go of that hurt and move on with your life? Have you even been able to forgive the person who hurt you?

The challenge for today: Ask God's help to forgive and forget. Make a conscious decision that every time that old grudge pops up in your mind, you will give it to God, forget about it, and move on.

"Bear with each other and forgive whatever grievances you may have against one another. Forgive as the Lord forgave you."
—Colossians 3:13

Don't Mess with the Mama

"THEY ARE NOT TAKING MY BABY. I don't care if Pharaoh himself demands that I hand him over—I won't do it!" Jochebed clutched her baby to her chest.

"Shhh!" Her husband was afraid the ever-present soldiers would hear her.

"Quit shushing me! I will save this boy! Either help me or get out of my way."

Her husband threw up his hands and stomped out of the house. Jochebed thought and prayed until a plan formed in her mind.

"Miriam, keep the baby quiet. I'll be back in a few minutes." She disappeared and returned later, her arms filled with reeds from the shore of the Nile River.

"Mama, what are you doing?" Miriam had never seen her mom like this. Jochebed ignored Miriam's questions and quickly wove the reeds into a little basket, which she coated with tar.

Then Jochebed took the baby and said, "Miriam, grab the basket and follow me." Jochebed led her daughter through town, dodging behind buildings anytime a soldier approached. When they got to the river, she kissed her baby and gently put him in the basket, tucking his favorite blanket around him. "I love you, sweet baby. You're in God's hands now," she whispered, gently pushing the basket into the river.

Jochebed walked home, shoulders sagging, while Miriam stayed to keep an eye on the basket. Everywhere Jochebed looked she saw reminders of her son. A few hours later, Miriam burst into the house. "Mama, come quickly! Pharaoh's daughter found the baby and she's going to keep him as her son. She wants a Hebrew woman to nurse him. You can take care of him. Hurry!"

BASED ON EXODUS 2:1–10

Reflections From The Heart

Action—that's what Jochebed was all about. She could have knelt beside her bed and prayed, pleading with God to keep her baby safe. In fact she probably did. But, then she didn't just get up and pace, wringing her hands, crying, "Woe is me, when is God going to do something?" God planted an idea in her mind about how she could help save Moses' life, and she leaped into action. What an example of faith and works walking hand in hand. I wonder if Jochebed realized that she was taking quite a chance by putting her plan into action? She risked her life and Miriam's life to keep her baby alive.

When I feel passionate about something, I usually pray earnestly, even pleading with God to handle the situation. As I read about Jochebed, I wonder how many times God may have wanted me to actively assist in solving the situation, but I was either too blind to his plan or too frightened by the risk of getting involved. It's so much easier to say, "*They* should do something about that," not realizing that I may be one of the *they* God wants to use.

The challenge for today: Be open to God's leading, be aware of any plans he places in your mind and heart, and be willing to take a risk and get involved. You may be God's tool.

"Be strong and courageous. Do not be terrified; do not be discouraged, for the LORD your God will be with you wherever you go."

—JOSHUA 1:9

Turning Corners

MOSES WAS BORN TO JEWISH SLAVES IN Egypt. He should have died as an infant, but his mother fought to give him a chance at life. He was raised as an Egyptian prince, but he ran away from his royal life in Egypt and ended up as a shepherd. Yet that wasn't the end, because God wasn't finished with Moses.

Moses strolled across the field where his sheep were grazing and approached a tree grove lined with bushes. Hot and tired, he dropped down on a rock and took a long drink of the cool water in his canteen. Something off to the left caught his eye. "What kind of bush is that? It's flaming red . . . no, wait, it's burning . . . but it's not burning up!"

"Moses, take off your shoes. You're on holy ground," a deep voice called out.

"What the . . . ." Moses scrambled to his feet but fell backward in his hurry to move away from the bush. "God? God is talking to me? Wait, OK. My shoes are off."

"I've heard the prayers of my people who want to be freed from slavery in Egypt. I want you to lead them to freedom."

"What? I can't do that. I'm just a shepherd. Who would listen to me? I can't even talk very well. I mean, I'm no public speaker. What if the people don't believe that you sent me?"

"I'll help you perform a miracle that will convince them."

"Well, uh, yes, but you know I have this stuttering problem."

"OK, I'll send along your brother, Aaron, as the public speaker; you just tell him what to say."

"Well, I don't know. . . ."

"Moses, get going."

Gulp. "OK."

BASED ON EXODUS 3:1–4:17

Reflections From The Heart

Moses didn't respond to God's call the way his mom had. Nope, Moses spewed out every excuse he could think of as to why God had chosen the wrong guy. God calmed his nerves and answered each of Moses' excuses.

Have you ever had a "burning bush" experience? A time when you looked around your church or community, saw a need, and felt a nudge in your heart. You could have leaped into action, but instead of stepping forward, you sat down until the feeling passed. Then you justified your lack of involvement with a myriad of stock excuses: "I'm so busy already. I've never tried doing something like that before. But, God, *she* could do a better job. I don't know how . . . ."

We read in Ephesians 2:10 that God gives each of us jobs to do. He also equips us with what we need to accomplish those tasks. God isn't the author of confusion, so he won't send us into a situation to flounder until we flop. What would that accomplish?

The challenge for today: Respond to that inner nudge to get involved, meet a need, and use the gifts and talents God has given you. Even if your gifts and talents are raw at the moment, they will certainly grow more polished with use.

"I can do everything through him who gives me strength."

—PHILIPPIANS 4:13

The Great Escape

GOD HAD DONE TEN INCREDIBLE MIRacles to convince Pharaoh to release the Israelites from their slavery. Then Moses marched them out of Egypt and into the desert. They thought they were home free . . . until they noticed a cloud of dust in the distance. As they watched it grow closer and larger, they realized it was Pharaoh's army. The Israelites were in the proverbial corner, with their backs against the waters of the Red Sea. Beginning a long-term pattern of behavior, instead of trusting God, they turned on Moses. "Pharaoh's army is coming to get us! We're dead meat!"

"Moses, why did you take us out of Egypt? We're going to die out here!"

"It's your fault we're in this mess. What are you going to do?"

Moses responded correctly and turned to God for help. "Just do what I say," God told him. Moses did. He climbed up on a rock at the water's edge and held his staff out over the water. Wind began to blow across the water, and the waves boiled and splashed. Suddenly the water blew into two waves that moved away from one another. All the water was contained in two huge walls, and the ground between them was dry.

"Get moving!" Moses shouted to the people. They walked through the Red Sea on dry ground—every last one of them. The Egyptians rode into the Red Sea after the Israelites, but, as soon as the whole army was between the water walls, Moses put his staff down. The water came crashing down, killing every Egyptian soldier, while the Israelites stood on the far shore and watched.

BASED ON EXODUS 14

 ## Reflections From The Heart

Imagine the faith of the first Israelite to step into the Red Sea and walk between those towering walls of water, trusting that God would hold the water back. Think about the feeling of wonder as the entire Israelite nation—millions of people—walked through the Red Sea on dry ground. Nothing is impossible for God! He takes care of his children, no matter what it takes.

Do you believe that last statement? Do you truly believe that God is taking care of you, protecting and guiding you through life? Or, do you sometimes feel overwhelmed and defeated, and God seems a million miles away? Most of us feel that way at one time or another. When you do, turn to stories like this one and hang your heart on the fact that God parted the Red Sea to protect his people. He loved them . . . and he loves you. Even on those days when you're overwhelmed with unpaid bills, a bad job (or no job), a husband who decides he doesn't want to be married anymore, or angry, rebellious teenagers—whatever your "Red Sea" might be—remember that God can handle it. Give it to him, trust him, and watch for the first ripples in the water.

The challenge for today: Don't ever give up hope. Look for the ways God is making his presence known in the difficulties of your life—even the small things he does that are easy to overlook. He may begin parting your Red Sea through something as simple as a phone call from a friend.

"Put your hope in God, for I will yet praise him, my Savior and my God." —PSALM 42:5

Cheeseburger Dreams

"MAMA, WHAT'S FOR DINNER?" ASKED a little Israelite boy.

"Creamed manna," Mama answered.

"No, not manna again. I'm sick of it. We eat it every single day for every single meal. Just forget it; I'm not hungry."

Mom watched her son stomp away. She didn't have an answer for his complaints, because she was just as frustrated as he was. What does a troubled mom do when she doesn't know what to do? She goes to see her best friend and pour out her troubles over a cup of coffee.

"Martha, my kids—" Before she could finish, her friend threw her hands up and spouted, "My family is rebelling against manna. I don't know what to do."

"Me either," said the first woman. "I guess I can't blame them. Remember the wonderful food we had in Egypt—all kinds of sweet, run-down-your-arm juicy fruits, and vegetables? And the meat . . . cooked until it was crusty on the outside and tender on the inside? Yummm."

Both women's mouths watered at the memory. "I know. Sometimes I actually dream about fruits and vegetables. Were we smart to follow Moses out of Egypt? Oh sure, we're not slaves anymore, but this is almost worse."

The first woman slammed her coffee cup on the table. "We struggle to stay alive, we have no homes, we wouldn't have food at all if it weren't for manna—and we're all sick of that. Maybe we should have stayed in Egypt."

BASED ON EXODUS 16

Reflections From The Heart

The Israelites had a history of being blind to God's provision. When they did see it, they were generally dissatisfied with what he gave them and how he cared for them. They wanted more.

Can you relate? Perhaps you're driving a perfectly good three-year-old car, but many of your neighbors have shiny new automobiles. Or, your functional family room furniture starts to look downright shabby compared to your friend's brand new top-of-the-line set. You feel dissatisfied because you don't have what someone else has, instead of being thankful for what you have and for how God is taking care of you. Come on, you know what I'm talking about. What's your "manna"? What are you whining about?

The challenge for today: Look around at all God has given you. Make a list of the everyday blessings that you may take for granted. Need a jump-start? How about good health, warm clothes, daily food, good friends, a free country? Realize how

God cares for you and provides for you, and be thankful. Stop complaining about what you *don't* have and celebrate what you *do* have.

"Enter his gates with thanksgiving and his courts with praise; give thanks to him and praise his name." —PSALM 100:4

Booster Friends

"JOSHUA, CALL YOUR SOLDIERS!" MOSES shouted. "The Amalekites are surrounding us!" Moses had led the Israelites for a long time. The people respected him and trusted his leadership because they knew that God spoke directly to him. Joshua, who commanded the Israelite army, quickly obeyed Moses and called his soldiers to fight the Amalekites, Israel's worst enemy.

The next morning Moses stood on the top of a big hill and held up the staff of God. Meanwhile, Joshua's army fought, hand to hand, fist to fist, spear to spear. The battle grew more and more fierce. The Amalekite army was big and strong and had crushed all armies that crossed their path. But Joshua's army fought with passion, and, amazingly, they were winning.

Late in the day, Moses tired and his arms began to droop. "This staff feels like it weighs a ton. I just can't hold it up any longer." His arms sank to his sides, and the battle swung in the Amalekites favor. When Moses raised his arms, the Israelites stormed back.

"Help me!" Moses cried.

Aaron and Hur ran to Moses and stood on either side of him. They each held one of his arms up high in the air, and Joshua's army won.

The Israelites slapped each other on the back and cheered their victory. Moses celebrated, too, but he knew that the battle couldn't have been won without the teamwork of Aaron, Hur, and Joshua seeking the power of God.

BASED ON EXODUS 17:8–16

 ## Reflections From The Heart

Teamwork rules! In this story, each man had a job to do, and he did it. Moses' job was to hold his arms up high and pray for the soldiers. Joshua's job was to lead the soldiers into battle. Aaron and Hur were important boosters in the whole plan; without them assisting Moses by holding his arms, who knows what would have happened? Apparently none of the four men got into a snit, wishing they had someone else's job or position.

Are you an out-front person who has gifts and talents to be the star of the show? Or, are you a backstage person who plays a supporting role, and without whom the show would never go on? Are you happy with where you are? Do you willingly do your part to make sure that jobs get done? Do you complain about the players in the other positions? Are you jealous of them?

The challenge for today: Understand that it takes a team working together to accomplish almost anything. Remember that there are no small parts. Know your job, your talents, and your gifts and perform to the very best of your ability, in concert with others.

"A cord of three strands is not quickly broken." —ECCLESIASTES 4:12

Good-bye "Wonder Woman"

"WHY CAN'T THESE PEOPLE GET ALONG with one another?" Moses asked. "God has performed miracle after miracle for them. Time after time he has protected them and given me specific information to guide them. It shouldn't be that hard to get along with each other. I'm spending all my time settling their arguments and fights that I don't even have time for my own life!" Moses was exhausted and frustrated, but he didn't know any other way to handle the problems of the Israelite people.

Then, one day his father-in-law, Jethro, came to visit. As the two men settled down to chat, a man knocked on the door. "Moses, we need help," the man said. "This guy stole some of my sheep . . ." Moses sighed and went to solve the problem.

When he returned, Jethro was waiting. "Why are you spending your time solving every piddling problem these people come up with?"

"Well, someone has to do it, or they would be at each other's throats all the time."

"You're wearing yourself out, and you aren't going to be any good to anybody. Let me give you some advice: Continue to be the people's representative before God, but find some capable, wise men to be judges over the people. Divide the people into groups of one thousand, one hundred, fifty, and ten, and appoint judges over those groups. Let the judges solve their problems. If an issue is too big for the judges, then they can come to you. But, you shouldn't have to handle every little thing that comes up." Jethro was gentle, but firm. "You need to delegate, my boy."

Moses thought that Jethro's plan made sense, so he did exactly what Jethro suggested . . . and it worked!

BASED ON EXODUS 18

 Reflections From The Heart

OK, Wonder Woman, listen and learn from Jethro's advice to Moses. You don't have to be all things to all people. Let go! Wonder Woman only exists in the cartoons!

Do you get caught up in trying to be the perfect wife, mom, friend, church member, employee . . . and whatever else you're involved in? Then, when you are completely exhausted and frustrated because you're not living up to your own expectations, do you beat yourself up and feel like a failure? Stop it!

God gave Moses some awesome gifts. But, he also gave gifts to the other Israelites and Moses wasn't giving them a chance to use their gifts because he was trying to do everything himself.

Jethro simply advised Moses to back off and let others help him by exercising their gifts. It was good for him and good for them.

Now think about yourself. Make a list of things you believe you are really good at. What do you really enjoy doing? Then think about all the other things that aren't your specialties, but you keep doing them anyway. Are there other people who could handle those responsibilities, and who would if you let them? Do you need to let go of some duties?

The challenge for today: Look at your God-given talents and interests and blend those with your nonnegotiable responsibilities, such as being a wife and mom. Give your best to those, delegate other duties, and let go of the "gotta-be-Wonder-Woman" thing.

"In Christ we who are many form one body, and each member belongs to all the others. We have different gifts, according to the grace given us." —ROMANS 12:5–6

The First Bull in a China Shop

GOD CALLED MOSES TO MT. SINAI FOR A special meeting. He gave Moses information to share with the Israelites—rules on how to treat him and others. God had a lot to say; the Israelites, at the foot of Mt. Sinai, got tired of waiting for Moses to return. "Aaron, we don't think Moses is coming back," some of them complained. "Maybe he fell in a ravine and died. We're tired of waiting."

"Yeah, we want a god we can see—not some mysterious God that meets with Moses by himself," the people insisted.

Aaron wasn't sure what to do. He didn't really have any authority, but it was kind of nice to have the people coming to him with their requests, even though he didn't have a clue about how to handle them. The people's complaints escalated, so Aaron frantically formulated a plan. "OK, bring me your gold jewelry, gold vases . . . any gold you can find." Aaron tossed all the gold into a pot and melted it. Then he shaped it into a calf and said, "Here you go, folks. This is the god that brought you out of Egypt!"

"All right! A god we can see. Let's party!" For days the people ate, danced, and sang. They bowed before their calf god and worshipped it.

God saw what they were doing and he was mad! He wanted to kill them—to wipe out everyone who had betrayed him. Moses begged him to give the people another chance, so God let Moses go down and handle the situation. Moses melted the calf, and he ground the gold into dust. Then he poured the dust over water and made the people drink it.

BASED ON EXODUS 32

 Reflections From The Heart

You may be able to identify with the Israelites' impatience. Perhaps you repeatedly have brought a situation to God, but after months or years, you still are waiting for his action or response. It's hard to hang in there sometimes, isn't it? We are tempted to take matters into our own hands and forge ahead like a bull in a china shop, with much the same results—precious things broken, crushed, and destroyed. We especially damage our own relationship with God. Pulling our trust or allegiance from him and placing it somewhere else is dangerous and only results in problems.

It would be so much easier if God operated on our timetable, wouldn't it? But, the fact of the matter is he doesn't—he sees the bigger picture and has a definite plan. So it is best to trust him.

During those days, weeks, months, and yes, even years of trust, we learn the most about him, and our faith grows stronger.

The challenge for today: Don't impatiently take matters into your own hands. Believe that God hears your prayers and is working in the situation, even if you can't see obvious evidence of his work right now. Trust him and stay true to him.

"He who trusts in himself is a fool, but he who walks in wisdom is kept safe." —PROVERBS 28:26

Unexpected Sources

BALAAM WAS FEELING MIGHTY IMPOR-tant as he rode his little donkey to King Balak's palace. After all, the king had offered him a lot of money to put a curse on the Israelites. Even if God didn't want him to curse them, it was quite an honor to be noticed by King Balak. Balaam was lost in his thoughts until the donkey veered off the road.

"What in the world is wrong with you, you crazy animal?" Balaam screamed. He smacked his little donkey with a stick while he yanked and tugged her back on the road. "Now, get going!" Balaam climbed back on the frightened animal and they trotted off down the road.

A few minutes later, the donkey leaned hard into a stone wall, crushing Balaam's foot and leg against it. "Oww, my leg! Stupid animal!" He again took a stick to the donkey. Limping, Balaam pulled her away from the wall.

The trip was uneventful for a while, and Balaam thought they would make it to King Balak's palace before sundown. But all of a sudden, the donkey lay down in the middle of the road. Balaam tumbled off to the side, screaming louder than ever. He beat the animal, until the donkey suddenly spoke. "What have I done to deserve these beatings?"

Balaam was so shocked that he dropped his stick. "Did you just speak to me?" he whispered, thinking he must be losing his mind. Quickly recovering, he shouted, "I punished you because you made me look like a fool. In fact, if I had a sword with me, I would have killed you by now!"

Suddenly, the Lord let Balaam see what the donkey had been seeing all day—the powerful angel of the Lord standing in the middle of the road with his sword drawn, and he didn't look very happy. "You should be thanking your donkey. Three times I would have killed you if she hadn't stopped or gone off the road. You are disobeying God by going to curse the Israelites for King Balak. It was my job to stop you."

Balaam dropped the stick, thanked God for the little donkey, and promised to obey God always.

BASED ON NUMBERS 22

 ## Reflections From The Heart

God told Balaam not to go to King Balak. The king wanted Balaam to curse, and thus help defeat, God's people, but God did-n't want him to have any part of it. However, Balaam got caught up in the money King Balak was offering (it's often money that trips us up, isn't it?), and he managed to justify his trip to the king. God had to stop him. Now, the first time the donkey ran off the road, Balaam could have realized that God was sending him a message. He didn't. The second time he certainly might have noticed that things weren't going well. He didn't. The third time, well . . . that didn't work either. He was so dense that God had to spell it out for him.

OK, confession time. Are you sometimes as dense as Balaam? I sure am. I'm the Queen of Justification, and when I make up my mind that I am going to do something, I can come up with dozens of reasons why it's OK and isn't hurting anyone. On a good day, I can even make it look like a good idea. God may even warn me through a "donkey"—a car that won't start, or a child with a temperature of 103—but I stubbornly keep on going. Can you identify?

How does God get your attention? If his guidance comes from unexpected sources, do you pay attention or do you justify it away? We usually know the right thing to do (or not do), just as Balaam did, so when God throws roadblocks our way, we should step back and evaluate. If Balaam had done that, he would have saved himself a lot of trouble.

The challenge for today: Stop justifying. Stay close to God and pay attention to the subtle ways he guides and leads you.

"I will instruct you and teach you in the way you should go; I will counsel you and watch over you." —PSALM 32:8

The Walls Fall Down

J OSHUA STOOD ON A BLUFF LOOKING OUT over the beautiful countryside of the promised land. "Joshua, I'm giving this land to you and your people," God said, "starting with the city of Jericho. It's yours."

"Did you say Jericho? Have you seen the big walls around that city? Do you know about the fighting men who live there? How can we possibly take that city?" Joshua knew his Israelite men were no match for the soldiers of Jericho.

"Just do what I tell you and the city is yours," God said. Joshua listened closely as God laid out the plan of attack. It was crazy. It lacked military strategy. They would look silly to the men of Jericho. If it worked, however, no one would doubt that they had captured the city by God's power, not their own.

When Joshua told the Israelites that God was going to help them capture Jericho, they immediately started celebrating, "Ha! We're gonna kick some Jericho butt!" "Yeah, they won't know what hit them. Whoowee are we gonna rub their noses in it!"

"Hang on, guys," Joshua interrupted. "God has a plan. We are to march around the city of Jericho once a day for six days . . . but we can't say even one word. On the seventh day, we march around seven times. The priests blow their horns, we shout, and the walls fall down. Simple."

"What? We're going to look like fools. The men of Jericho will laugh us out of the country. Are you sure you got the plan right?"

"I'm sure. Look, its God's way or the highway."

BASED ON JOSHUA 6

 ## Reflections From The Heart

The Israelites did obey God's plan. Joshua led them around the city once a day for six days, and not one man said a word, and yes, the men of Jericho did think they were crazy. They didn't take the Israelites seriously until the seventh day when Joshua led them around the city seven times, the horns blared, the people shouted, and . . . the walls fell!

I wonder what would have happened if the Israelites had decided to take a little shortcut—if they marched all around the city for three days but only halfway around for the next three days. Then, on the seventh day, they circled the city four times and shouted on the fifth time. Do you think they would have been successful? I don't. I think following God's instructions to the very best of their abilities was important to their success, because that showed respect and honor for him.

Now, there may have been a problem if the Israelites expected to see some little successes before the seventh trip around on the seventh day. When nothing was changed from day to day—the walls stood thick and strong, the men of Jericho still made fun of them, and God wasn't waving "You Go!" banners in the sky, do you think they may have been tempted to give up? Perhaps they wondered if Joshua had misunderstood God's directions.

Regardless, they stuck with the plan. They obeyed God's instructions and trusted God to do what he said he was going to do. That obedience paid off.

The challenge for today: Don't take shortcuts in your faith. In the Scriptures, God has laid out very clear instructions for how to know him better and how to relate to other people. Just do it—even if it sometimes seems like you go a long time with no obvious growth or results. Trust and obey.

"If you love me, you will obey what I command." —JOHN 14:15

Listen to the Woman!

DEBORAH WAS A POWERFUL WOMAN. As a judge in Israel, she sat under a palm tree and the Israelites came to ask her to solve their problems. She had a close relationship with God and she constantly sought his help. Sometimes he even gave her instructions for the Israelites, which she passed on to them.

One time the Lord gave Deborah a message for Barak. "God has heard our cries for rescue from Sisera. That wicked Canaanite has pushed us down and persecuted us for twenty years and God has had enough."

"Praise God!" Barak cried. Sisera treated the Israelites horribly. He was a nasty, evil man, and Barak was thrilled to know they would be free of him.

"Call together ten thousand of your soldiers. God will lure Sisera to the Kishon River and God will help you defeat him there," Deborah instructed, turning to head back to her palm tree.

"Whoa, Nellie. Me? I'm supposed to face off against the evil, sneaky Sisera? I don't think so." Barak backed away. Deborah didn't say a word; she just stared him down. "OK, OK, I'll call my army and I'll go . . . but only if you go with me." Deborah was frustrated with this big, strong soldier, but she took a deep breath and calmly said, "Fine, I'll go with you. But that means that the honor of the victory over Sisera will go to a woman, not to you." Oddly enough, Barak didn't seem to care. He called his soldiers and, with Deborah by his side, they set out for the Kishon River.

The two armies started fighting and when Sisera saw that his army wasn't going to win, he ran away and hid in the tent of a woman named Jael. She waited until Sisera fell asleep; then, Jael grabbed a metal spike and drove it through Sisera's temple. Just as Deborah had predicted, a woman got the credit for killing God's enemy.

BASED ON JUDGES 4–5

 Reflections From The Heart

I can hear some of you whispering, "Men never listen to women." "Why didn't Barak just listen to Deborah?" Yeah, I have some of those same questions. But, let's not go there. Let's look at the positive side of this story: "You go, girl!" Deborah was a leader. She had an important job in Israel, and she must have been a very strong woman. She took her position seriously and apparently was a bit frustrated that Barak didn't show the strength she thought he should. Regardless of Barak's attitude, Deborah did what she had to do for God's enemy to be defeated.

For some of us, being in a position of leadership is rather frightening. We worry that we might make a mistake or a bad choice, or that people won't want to follow us. We even worry that we might mess up God's work. I once heard a speaker say, "Who do you think you are? Do you assume that you are so powerful, so important, that you could mess up the work of the Creator of the universe?" Get over yourself, honey. If God places you in a position of leadership in your home, church, ladies group, or community government, trust him to guide you, and allow yourself to make mistakes and learn from them. Take the responsibility seriously and do the work God places before you. One of a leader's most important tasks is leading by example, just as Deborah did. It's easy to tell people, "Do as I say," but its another thing entirely to lead with, "Do as I do."

The challenge for today: If you have an opportunity to be a leader, grab it and run with it. You just might end up doing something awesome for God.

"Those who hope in the LORD will renew their strength. They will soar on wings like eagles; they will run and not grow weary, they will walk and not be faint." —ISAIAH 40:31

Just Making Sure

GIDEON WAS AMAZED. "GOD WANTS ME to rescue Israel from the Midianites? The mighty Midianites who steal our crops and herds? They kill our strongest men or beat them within an inch of life." Gideon stared at the angel delivering this message from God. "Have you looked at me? Have you looked at my tribe? We're the smallest and weakest of the whole nation, and I'm the smallest and weakest of my family. Wanna rethink this?" Gideon couldn't believe that God would ask him to do this job when there were bigger, more powerful men in Israel. But the angel of God assured him that he was the man.

"OK, don't get mad, God, but I have to make sure about this. If you really want me to rescue Israel, do this for me. I'll put some wool on the floor tonight. If the wool is soaking wet in the morning, but the ground all around is dry, then I'll know that you're going to help me." The next morning Gideon couldn't even squeeze all the water out of the wool.

"Now, don't get upset, but let me try this once more. If I've got the story right then this time, let the wool stay dry while the ground all around it is wet. Then I'll believe that you really want me to do this." Early the next morning, Gideon checked and the wool was dry as a bone, but the ground all around it was wet.

BASED ON JUDGES 6:36–40

 ## Reflections From The Heart

This system of testing God's guidance worked for Gideon. He was a young man who had been given a monumental task, and he needed assurance that God was going with him into the battle. But it probably isn't the best way for us to discover God's will. It leaves too much room for misinterpretation. It certainly would be easier if God wrote his instructions across the sky, wouldn't it? Part of the journey of knowing God, however, involves studying his Word and spending time in prayer. That's how we get to know him and learn to discern his will. It's not always easy, but it is always worth it.

Are you willing to make the effort to know the heart and wisdom of God? Or do you approach God's guidance like this: "If you want me to go to church today, then make all the stoplights green." Or "If you want me to talk to my friend about that problem between us, then have her call me." Here's one of my favorites: "If you want me to get into college, then let me ace all my high school finals; and just to make sure of your plan, I won't study for them." Russian roulette guidance is not the best way to plan your life.

The challenge for today: Seek God's guidance through studying his Word, spending time conversing with him, and listening to the counsel of godly friends and mentors, instead of taking your guidance through circumstances.

"Trust in the LORD *with all your heart and lean not on your own understanding; in all your ways acknowledge him, and he will make your paths straight."* —PROVERBS 3:5–6

"My God Is So Big!"

AFTER THE SECOND WOOL INCIDENT, confirming Gideon's call to rescue the Israelites from the Midianites, he called together his army. They were thirty-two thousand strong and ready to fight.

"You've got too many soldiers," God informed Gideon. "If you defeat the enemy with all these soldiers, the men will boast that they won without my help." So, Gideon offered to let any man go home who was the least little bit afraid. Twenty-two thousand men left.

It will be harder, that's for sure, but we can win with ten thousand determined men, Gideon thought, though his confidence was wavering a bit.

"You've still got too many soldiers," God said. He told Gideon how to pare down the number even more. Any man who drank river water by cupping it in his hands stayed; everyone else went home.

"Three hundred men? You want me to fight the Midianites with three hundred men?" Gideon was a little nervous. But he and his little army followed God's instructions—and won—by God's power, not their own.

BASED ON JUDGES 7

 ## Reflections From The Heart

God certainly made a point here, didn't he? He committed himself to help Gideon's army defeat the Midianites, but he wanted everyone to know that the victory came through him; not because Gideon had a massive number of soldiers.

How does this lesson translate in your life? You can have victory in any area of life—with God's power. It's actually freeing, because you don't need an Ivy League education, make a zillion dollars a year, have a supermodel's figure, or possess the brilliance of an Einstein . . . all you need is God. When he gives you a job to do, he will equip you with his power to accomplish it. Believe it.

The challenge for today: Don't spend time fretting about what you can't accomplish because of what you don't have. Start moving forward, and allow God to accomplish what he wishes through you. Remember to give him the credit.

"I pray that out of his glorious riches he may strengthen you with power through his Spirit in your inner being, so that Christ may dwell in your hearts through faith." —EPHESIANS 3:16–17

Loyal to the End

RUTH QUICKLY LEARNED THAT BEING married took some getting used to. Oh, Ruth didn't mind the housework and cooking, but being part of her new husband's family was different than she had expected. They were from Judah, so their customs seemed strange, and they worshipped God, which was new to her. But, all in all, Ruth was happy. She even liked her mother-in-law, Naomi.

Tragedy struck, however, when Ruth's husband died. She was heartbroken, for herself and for Naomi, who had now lost her husband and both of her sons. When Naomi decided to return to Judah, Orpah, Naomi's other daughter-in-law, and Ruth chose to go along.

"No, go back home to your families," Naomi told them. "You can marry again. My family is in Judah, I'll be all right."

But, Ruth and Orpah refused to let her make the trip alone. Not far into the journey, however, Orpah began missing her parents, so Naomi sent her home. Ruth still insisted on staying with

Naomi. She said, "Your family will be my family and your God will be my God."

Life in Bethlehem wasn't easy. Ruth provided food for the two of them by picking up grain that the field workers dropped. It was backbreaking work, but she didn't complain. "A generous man named Boaz owns the field," she told Naomi. "He asked the workers to drop extra grain for me."

"Ruth is a nice girl," people told Boaz. "She left her own family and she works hard to take care of her mother-in-law." Ruth and Boaz soon were married and became the proud parents of a baby boy, who would be an ancestor of Jesus Christ.

BASED ON THE BOOK OF RUTH

Reflections From The Heart

Ruth's loyalty and love for Naomi is legendary. Ruth's words of commitment are even commonly quoted at weddings. Then the bride and groom make a similar promise, vowing to stick together, no matter what hardships life brings. Down the road, however, when the bumps get big and the fun wears thin, too often the loyalty is shaken.

When my husband recently announced that his company wanted to move us to another part of the country, I confess I didn't respond like Ruth. I thought about the family and friends I would be leaving behind. I focused on how I would miss our church and the ministries in which I am involved. I even mourned for the grocery store where I am comfortable shopping. (Yeah, I'm faithful to my grocery store.) Loyalty and commitment to my husband, however, were pretty far down on my list. Later I realized I lacked support for my husband because I was so concerned about my comfort. Moving to another part of the country was frightening. It would disrupt my life.

Consider Ruth's life. She made a commitment to Naomi that involved leaving her family and homeland for a life that promised to be tough. Ruth stuck it out and God rewarded her. He gave her another husband and a child who was an ancestor of Jesus Christ.

Looking at Ruth's life raises questions about my own. I wonder if I've missed out on some awesome blessings because of my loyalty to my own comfort. And I wonder, have you?

The challenge for today: When the opportunity presents itself, choose the way of loyalty and faithfulness to God's plan and let go of what's comfortable.

"Where you go I will go, and where you stay I will stay. Your people will be my people and your God my God." —RUTH 1:16

Longing for a Baby's Cry

HANNAH WANTED A CHILD. SHE LONGED to hold her own baby in her arms, sing him to sleep, teach him to walk, and laugh at his first words. But Hannah had no children, even though she had been married to Elkanah for years. Her husband didn't mind, but his other wife, Peninnah, loved to remind Hannah of her failure to bear children.

"Useless, that's what you are. What good is a wife who can't give her husband a child?" Peninnah was ruthless. She was determined to be the "favored" wife, seldom missing a chance to brag about her many children.

Elkanah was caught in the middle of his wives' struggle. "I love you, Hannah, and if you have children that will be wonderful. But if you don't, well, I just don't care." Hannah didn't believe him; she bought into Peninnah's accusations. Plus, she truly wanted a baby.

One year Hannah accompanied Elkanah to Shiloh to worship God. Kneeling in the temple, she poured out her heart in prayer. "Please give me a son. If you do, I promise that I'll give him back to your service." The old priest in the temple saw Hannah talking to herself and thought she was drunk. "How dare you come into God's house under the influence!"

"But, I haven't been drinking. It's just that I want a baby very much. I was pleading with God to give me a child."

Hannah's prayer was answered when she gave birth to Samuel. True to her promise, she brought him to live at the temple with Eli, who taught Samuel how to be a priest of God.

BASED ON 1 SAMUEL 1

 Reflections From The Heart

Hannah was passionate about wanting a child. She begged God for a baby. Then, when she had a child, she gave him away. Notice that Hannah kept her promise. Her plea to God wasn't a foxhole prayer to get out of a tough situation. After she got what she wanted, she didn't forget about her part of the bargain. That's not who Hannah was. She made a deal with God and, when he came through, she kept her promise.

How good is your word? When you tell someone that you will do something, do you follow through? Or do you sometimes try to justify your way out of a bargain? That's not good, my friend. Our friends and family need to know they can count on us, regardless of how busy we are or what else pops up in our lives.

59

What about your promises to God? You know what I'm talking about—those vows to start a daily devotional time, to build friendships with non-Christians, to seek to break a bad habit or to let go of a certain sin. You can justify and make excuses with your family and friends, but God sees the heart. You can't fool him.

The challenge for today: Don't make promises you don't plan to keep. Whether your agreement is with God or with another person, be true to your word. You'll be glad you did.

"The LORD detests lying lips, but he delights in men who are truthful."
—PROVERBS 12:22

Bigger Isn't Always Better

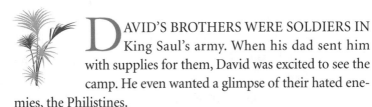DAVID'S BROTHERS WERE SOLDIERS IN King Saul's army. When his dad sent him with supplies for them, David was excited to see the camp. He even wanted a glimpse of their hated enemies, the Philistines.

As he entered the camp, David heard shouts from across the valley. "Hey chickens, send someone to fight me, if anyone is brave enough!" A nine-foot-tall Philistine giant flexed his muscles, as he shouted again, "Ain't your God powerful enough to help you win?"

No Israelite stepped forward. David asked the soldiers, "Are you guys gonna let that creep get away with making fun of you and God?"

"What are you doing here?" David's brother Eliab grabbed David's shoulder and whirled him around.

"I brought you supplies from Dad. How can you put up with that guy? Someone said that Goliath has shouted that twice a day for forty days. Why don't you stop him?"

"Go home you little show-off. You have no business here," Eliab shoved David aside.

David started to leave, but his heart pulled him back. He marched up to King Saul and said, "I'll fight that giant!"

At first King Saul was thrilled . . . then he took a closer look at the volunteer. "You're a kid! Goliath has been a soldier longer than you've been alive. What chance would you have against him?" But, David's eyes shone with determination. "OK," the king said, "but at least wear my armor. It will give you some protection."

David tried on the armor, but it was so heavy he couldn't walk, "Get me outta this!" he cried. Then he headed down the hill, picking up a few stones along the way.

When Goliath saw a kid coming, he was hopping mad. "Come 'ere you little twerp. I'm gonna feed you to the birds!" he growled. The Philistines erupted in laughter, sure that David would soon be bird food. Meanwhile, King Saul's soldiers were on their feet watching the action.

"You big creep," David shouted at Goliath. "You may be bigger than me. You may be stronger than me. But, I've got something you don't—I've got the power of God on my side!" He dropped a stone into his leather sling. Twirling it around over his head, David looked up into the giant's eyes and let the stone fly. It smacked into Goliath's forehead and the giant hit the ground.

"Yahoo!" King Saul's army cheered, "David won. The little guy won!"

BASED ON 1 SAMUEL 17

Reflections From The Heart

What's your Goliath? What looms in your life, controlling you and popping up daily? You would like to beat it once and for all, but it seems too big to handle. Do you doubt you ever could have victory over it? Perhaps your struggle is to lose weight, or to stop smoking. Maybe you battle a negative attitude, or an explosive temper, or an addiction. Whatever you would like to conquer probably seems so big and you feel so small. In the past, you may even have begun a plan of attack (usually on New Years Day, right?), but by January 3rd you're defeated once again.

So, what do you do? The reason that little ol' David could defeat big ol' Goliath was that David made use of God's power. He didn't try to cream the big guy in his own strength; he knew he wouldn't have a chance. David knew he was fighting God's enemy and that God would be on his side. So he called on that power and stepped out in confidence.

By calling on God's power to help us, we also can have victory. Jesus said that if we have faith the size of a mustard seed, we can tell a mountain to jump in the ocean, and it will. (Matthew 17:20). What amazing power is available to us. If only we would call on it.

The challenge for today: Remember the evidences of God's power as shared in Scripture. Also remember the evidences of God's power you've seen in your own life. Call on that power to battle your Goliath.

"My grace is sufficient for you, for my power is made perfect in weakness." —2 CORINTHIANS 12:9

Keepin' the Peace

STUBBORN FOOL, THOUGHT ABIGAIL AS she threw bread into baskets. *My husband just can't keep his mouth shut. . . . most selfish man in the world . . . rude . . . unkind . . .* Abigail could go on forever. Nabal was always making somebody angry and she was forever picking up the pieces. *This time he may have gone too far,* she thought. *He made King David mad—King David! For goodness' sake, we sing songs about his courage, power, and victories. He's our hero!*

Abigail plucked out a bad grape before plopping a bunch in a basket, "Would it have been so hard for him to give David's soldiers a little food? Oh no, my husband has to make a nasty comment about giving his food to a band of outlaws. Oh my, I know David is going to kill him."

Abigail stuffed bread into the last basket, climbed on a donkey and headed for David's camp. "Come on little donkey, go faster," she prodded. Just then Abigail saw a cloud of dust. It grew larger and larger, and soon she could make out King David and his soldiers—on the way to kill her husband.

When he was close enough Abigail called, "Sir, my husband is a fool. I didn't know about your request for food until it was too late. But, I've brought you some now. You've never done anything wrong, great King. Don't start now. Don't murder my husband; please forgive him."

"Thank you for stopping me from doing something wrong," David quietly answered. "I accept your food, and I'll let your husband live."

Abigail praised God that King David heard her request.

BASED ON 1 SAMUEL 25:1–35

Reflections From The Heart

Can you identify with Abigail? Do you often feel like you are cleaning up somebody else's mess? No doubt you do if you're a wife and mom. Abigail could have washed her hands of the whole mess and said, "Hubby, you're on your own this time." If she had, David probably would have killed Nabal. Abigail's efforts to be a peacemaker saved David from doing something he shouldn't and gave Nabal a chance to straighten up and fly right (he didn't).

If you're having coffee with someone and she starts ripping up another friend, how do you respond? Do you join in the attack? Do you listen quietly as you stretch duct tape across your mouth? Do you let your friend get her anger out of her system, then try to rationally talk her through the problem? In other words, are you part of the problem or part of the solution?

Being a peacemaker sets us apart in this day of road and office rage. Everyone gets upset with other people at one time or another, and we all handle it differently. But, those of us who claim Christ as Savior should be an example as to how to handle relationship problems. I know that isn't exactly what you want to hear when you're madder than a wet hen. But, you've probably heard the phrase, "Your life may be the only Bible some people ever read." Big responsibility, huh? Can people look at your life and see a peacemaker who acts with love and fairness toward others—an example of the character of God?

The challenge for today: Think before speaking, so that you don't leap into a rip-up-someone party. Look for ways to create peace in the lives of those around you. Help family and friends, as you help yourself, to focus on others instead of having a me-first attitude.

"God has called us to live in peace." —1 CORINTHIANS 7:15

Taking a Stand

ELIJAH WAS FED UP WITH THE ISRAELITES. "Make up your mind. If God is God, then worship him. If Baal is god, then worship him." The people were silent. "I'm the only prophet of God left, but Baal has 450 prophets," Elijah shouted. "I challenge them to a contest."

Elijah arranged a meeting on Mt. Carmel. Baal's prophets would build an altar to sacrifice a bull; Elijah would do the same. Then they each would call on their respective deity to send down fire and consume the sacrifice. Simple.

Good sport that he was, Elijah let the prophets of Baal go first. "Come on, Baal. Here's our altar. Send down fire and burn it up. Let's go, Baal. Here we go, Baal!"

Elijah sat down and watched the prophets dance around, shouting and begging. "Maybe Baal is in the bathroom. Or, maybe he's asleep—you'd better yell louder." He enjoyed making fun of them. Finally, Elijah got tired, "That's long enough. It's my turn now."

Elijah built his altar and put the bull on it. The prophets of Baal thought he was crazy when he dug a trench around the altar and poured four large jars of water over it. Then he dumped on four more jars. When he did it a third time, they were sure that altar would never burn. As water poured out of the trenches, Elijah stepped back and raised his eyes to heaven. "OK, God, show these guys your power," he calmly said. Fire immediately shot down from heaven and burned up the altar, the bull, and all the water! There was no doubt who the real God was.

BASED ON 1 KINGS 18:19–39

 Reflections From The Heart

Elijah forced the issue, didn't he? He was tired of people living on the fence, not taking a stand for or against God; trying to keep their feet in both worlds. The Israelites were afraid to openly deny Baal, as his prophets were powerful. Of course, they knew of God's power and they had a history with him, so they didn't want to deny him, either. But, as they found out, you can ride the fence for only so long.

Do you sometimes find yourself keeping one foot in the world and one foot in God's family? Why? When you hang out with non-Christians, do you try to fit in by compromising your standards and beliefs? Are you afraid of their reaction if they learn of your faith?

The Scriptures tell us that God is a jealous God who doesn't want to share your allegiance with anyone or anything else. As long as you stay on the fence, you will be a lukewarm Christian, at best. Read this story again and notice God's power. He sent fire that consumed a flooded altar. Don't you want that power working in your life? I do.

The challenge for today: Get off the fence and in the game. Jump into the Christian life with both feet. . . . Just do it!

"If the LORD is God, follow him; but if Baal is God, follow him."
—1 KINGS 18: 21

Silence Is Golden

ELIJAH HAD BEEN THROUGH SOME rough times. He needed some peace and quiet to recuperate. So he crawled into a cave and fell asleep.

"Elijah, what are you doing here?" A gentle voice woke him.

"O God, I've served you with all my strength, all my energy. But, I'm the only one of your prophets left alive. The people of Israel have broken their promises to you, and now they are trying to kill me, too." Elijah was at the end of his rope.

"Go out and stand before me on the mountain," God said. Elijah dragged his tired body outside the cave. A powerful wind began to blow. Trees were pulled out of the ground by their roots. Elijah clung to a rock to keep from blowing off the mountain himself. But, God wasn't in the wind.

After the wind, the earth shook, but God wasn't in the earthquake either. Next, fire roared down the mountain, but God wasn't in the fire. Elijah wondered what was going on. Then he heard a gentle whisper blowing across the mountainside. Elijah hid his face in his coat . . . and listened. God was in the whisper, and he assured Elijah that, even though it sometimes seemed like he was alone, he wasn't.

BASED ON 1 KINGS 19

 ## Reflections From The Heart

It's understandable that Elijah needed to get away for a while. Life gets pretty hectic sometimes and we all need a little rest and relaxation. What is most interesting about this event is how God spoke. Which of the natural events that Elijah witnessed would you have expected to hold God's presence? The powerful windstorm? How about the incredible earthquake? The fire? In the Old Testament, fire is often associated with God's presence. But God didn't speak through any of those powerful, awesome, frightening means. He spoke in a whisper. That could have been easy to miss, couldn't it? Elijah had to listen carefully.

How are you at finding quiet times in your life? Do you take time for silence, with no children clamoring, no TV or radio blaring—just stillness as you wait to hear God's voice? God isn't going to compete for your attention. He will wait for the quiet moments. To create those opportunities, you may need to get up very early in the morning, before the little ones wake up. You may need to turn off the TV or radio in the afternoon, or spend your lunch hour alone with God. Whatever it takes, it's important to build quiet times into your life. Otherwise, how can you hear God speak?

The challenge for today: Work some quiet time into your life, and listen for the voice of God.

"Be still, and know that I am God." —PSALM 46:10

71

Taking Care
of Others

THE LITTLE WOMAN OF SHUNEM WAS known for her generous spirit. She took food to the needy and invited people to stay in her home. She was one of those people who constantly noticed ways to help others. For example, some time ago she met the prophet Elisha when he passed through town. She invited him to her home for dinner. Then she noticed that he needed a place to stay, so she offered her guest room. After that, every time Elisha came through Shunem, he stayed at her home.

One day, after Elisha left, she was cleaning when she got an idea. "Honey," she called to her husband, "why don't we build a room for Elisha? He would have his own place where he could leave his things. He would know that he always has a place to stay in Shunem. What do you think?"

Her husband wasn't a bit surprised by her suggestion; he knew his wife. He drew up plans and the room was quickly built, decorated, and furnished. The next time Elisha came to town, he knocked on her door, expecting to be ushered to the guest room as usual. Instead, his hostess welcomed him with, "We have a surprise for you." When she showed him the new room, Elisha thanked God for the kind woman and her generous husband.

BASED ON 2 KINGS 4:8–11

 Reflections From The Heart

Do you think this woman ever had dust bunnies under her bed, fingerprints on the wall, or milk circles on the countertop? If so, they didn't seem to bother her. She had the gift of hospitality. She generously invited Elisha to stay with her whenever he came to town, and ended up building him his own room. Apparently money was no object.

OK, put the money topic aside. Do you know people who love to entertain? They have people into their home all the time, and it just isn't an issue if newspapers are stacked on the couch or if they have only store-bought cookies and ice cream to serve. They just enjoy entertaining. Now, I enjoy entertaining, too. When new families move into the neighborhood or visit our church, I love to have them over for dinner—after I dust, vacuum, paint the hallway, and bake a fancy cake with butter-cream frosting. So I don't often have people over.

Are you, by any chance, hospitality challenged, as I am? Do you get hung up on the idea that everything has to be perfect before you can enjoy the company of friends, or the opportunity to make new ones? My friend, we have to get over this.

73

The challenge for today: Learn from the woman of Shunem. Enjoy people—don't focus on dust or fingerprints or the ever-present newspapers—just enjoy spending time with people. Share your home, share your smile, share your heart.

"Do not forget to do good and to share with others, for with such sacrifices God is pleased." —HEBREWS 13:16

This May Be the Reason

ESTHER ENJOYED A YEAR OF PAMPERING and beauty treatments, fine food and ladies-in-waiting. Then, from hundreds of beautiful girls, the king chose her to be queen. That meant an easier life for the young orphan who had lived with her cousin, Mordecai, since her parents died. She settled into the royal life and everyone loved the gentle queen, who was beautiful on the inside as well as the outside.

A problem arose, however, when Haman, the king's honored noble, got mad at Mordecai. Everyone bowed when Haman passed by, except Mordecai, who refused to bow to anyone but God. Enraged, Haman got King Xerxes to order that all the Jews in the land be killed. Things looked bad.

"This may be very the reason you became queen," Mordecai whispered. He could see the fear in young Queen Esther's eyes.

"Our people are going to be killed, and you are our only hope. Remember, you're a Jew, too. Don't think for a minute that you will escape the massacre."

Esther turned away. "Mordecai, no one knows I'm Jewish, not even the king. I don't know what he would do if he found out."

Esther could go to the king and reveal Haman's evil plan . . . and her own Jewishness. She would be risking her life, however, because anyone who entered the king's presence without being summoned could be killed. Esther took a deep breath and said, "Have our people fast and pray for me for three days. Then I'll go to the king. If I die, then I die."

BASED ON THE BOOK OF ESTHER

 ## Reflections From The Heart

Esther may have thought her life was finally settling down after being orphaned and then living with a cousin who wasn't especially wealthy. But, just when things got comfy, she had to make an extremely difficult decision. Whichever choice she made, she would be putting her life on the line. It looked like a no-win situation.

I remember as a teenager becoming passionate about something and stepping forward to take a stand for my beliefs. I risked my reputation before my peers—tough for a teenager. I did lose a few friends, but on the positive side, those of us who took a stand motivated others to come forward, too. I truly felt that I made a difference. It was a good feeling.

Do you believe in anything enough to put your life on the line for it? OK, in North America today, we don't often face life or death kinds of decisions, such as Esther did. But what about taking a stand on something that risks your popularity, or your standing in the community, or other people's opinions of you? We all face those on a regular basis. We have the opportunity to take a stand for God, for the rights of children, or for abused women. The list could be endless.

The challenge for today: Take a risk by taking a stand. You may be called to take a stand for God in your community or for some individual cause that has wrapped itself around your heart. Take a lesson from Esther; fast and pray, then step forward in faith.

"The LORD is my strength and my shield; my heart trusts in him, and I am helped."—PSALM 28:7

No Compromise

DANIEL, SHADRACH, MESHACH, AND Abednego were captured and dragged to Babylon. The Jewish boys were given Babylonian names and put in a select training program to serve in the Babylonian king's palace. They were taught the Babylonian language and literature, and were treated to the best the king had to offer. Not bad for slaves, eh?

The problem was the food. It violated the Jewish dietary laws. Perhaps it had been offered to idols before being given to the boys. "We can't eat this stuff," Daniel whispered to his buddies.

"Right . . . why?" one of them whispered back.

"God forbids some of it. It's unclean. We'll be disobeying God," Daniel explained. "I'm not going to eat it. Are you with me?"

They knew that Daniel was right, so they agreed. "Sir," Daniel approached the guard, "my friends and I wish to eat vegetables and water instead of this food." The rest of the boys dropped their muffins in amazement.

"The king ordered this food for you. If you four boys look pale and weak, while the others are strong and healthy, he'll have my head!"

"Just let us try it for ten days. If you notice any difference between us and the other boys, then we'll eat the king's food for the rest of the training time." Daniel could be very convincing. At the end of the ten days, Daniel and his friends looked better and stronger than the other boys did! So, for the rest of the program, they had vegetables and water.

BASED ON DANIEL 1

Reflections From The Heart

Oh, those difficult times when temptation rears its ugly head. Daniel wasn't very old when this situation developed. Yet he showed an impressive amount of maturity in dealing with temptation and in taking a stand that could have been very unpopular. He did so because he wasn't willing to compromise his beliefs or his relationship with God.

Who among us can't understand a temptation story related to food? Sigh. Well, how do you handle temptation? If you're like me, you can be very strong in some areas, but in others you have the backbone of a wet noodle. How do you develop more strength in those areas where temptation seems to get the best of you? Do what Daniel did. Come up with a plan—think ahead so you're prepared to handle temptations when they arise. Seek God's strength and the support of friends. Consider the long-range implications of giving in to temptation; is it worth the immediate gratification?

The challenge for today: Write down one temptation with which you struggle. Stay close to God and draw on his strength, develop a support group to help you, and overcome that temptation.

"Come near to God and he will come near to you." —JAMES 4:8

Hot Time in the Old Town Tonight!

KING NEBUCHADNEZZAR HAD ORDERED that everyone in the kingdom bow down to his gold statue, and everyone did, except Shadrach, Meshach, and Abednego. So he made examples of them.

"Fire up the furnace!" King Nebuchadnezzar yelled. "Make it seven times hotter than it's ever been. We're frying some Jewish boys tonight!"

Shadrach, Meshach, and Abednego calmly stood by and watched the guards throw more fuel in the furnace. They should have been shaking in their boots, but they weren't.

"Have you changed your minds, fellas? Want to bow before my big gold statue now?" King Nebuchadnezzar asked.

"Sir, we mean no disrespect to you. But we will not bow to anyone or anything except our God. If that means you have to throw us in this furnace, then so be it. Our God will take care of us," the boys replied.

"Yeah, right . . . your God," the king snarled. "Throw 'em in!" he ordered. When the guard opened the furnace door, the blast of air was so hot that it killed him on the spot. Another guard shoved the boys into the flames and slammed the door. The king settled back to watch the boys burn.

King Nebuchadnezzar strained to see through the flames. He couldn't quite make it out . . . wait a minute, was he seeing four people . . . walking around in the blazing hot furnace? The fourth looked like a god or something. "How many men did we throw in the furnace?" he asked.

"Three, your highness."

"Get them out here," he ordered. Shadrach, Meshach, and Abednego walked out of the blazing furnace, unharmed. They didn't even smell like smoke.

"We knew our God would take care of us," they said to the king.

King Nebuchadnezzar took a deep breath. He knew that he couldn't ignore what he had just seen, "Praise to the God of Shadrach, Meshach, and Abednego. He protected his servants who trusted in him!" King Nebuchadnezzar shouted.

BASED ON DANIEL 3

 Reflections From The Heart

Faith is the bottom line in the story of Shadrach, Meshach, and Abednego. They knew that God would protect them, so they were willing to jump out of the frying pan and into the fire. They knew that God wouldn't leave them alone. The boys honored God by refusing to bow down to the king's statue, and they knew that God would honor them in return.

Of course it's easy to trust God when life is cool and calm, but do you trust him enough to allow yourself to be thrown into a blazing hot furnace? Do you believe that he will protect you during those difficult times? What are your furnace times of life? When the doctor says the biopsy was positive, or your husband says he's leaving? When your child is lost in drugs, or financial stability is crumbling around you? Is your God powerful enough to get you through these tough times?

Remember what God is like. Read through the Bible and notice how he takes care of his children. He parts waters to keep them safe, sends food from heaven when they're hungry, shuts the lions' mouths, raises the dead back to life, and makes blind men see. Look at his awesome power. He's worthy of your complete trust.

The challenge for today: Learn to trust God more fully. Granted, this is scary. Start by trusting him with a small thing, and when you see him honor that, move to something bigger. It's a journey. Enjoy it.

"Great is our LORD and mighty in power; his understanding has no limit." —PSALM 147:5

The Longest Night

"WHY IS KING DARIUS GIVING DANIEL so much responsibility?" complained the king's other administrators. "He's a slave, he shouldn't be a ruler—especially over us." The jealous men put their heads together and came up with a way to get Daniel in trouble . . . big trouble.

"This guy is squeaky clean. We can't find anything to use against him. All he does is work and pray," they said.

"Wait a minute, did you say, 'pray'? That's it." Yep, Daniel's prayer life was just the thing they needed. They tricked King Darius into signing a law that for the next thirty days people could pray to no one but the king himself. Disobeying meant death in the lions' den.

Daniel heard about the law, but his devotion to God was stronger than fear of punishment. So he continued his habit of praying three times a day, right in front of his open window—just what his enemies were hoping for. They ran straight to King Darius shouting, "Daniel broke the law. Punish him!" King

Darius knew he had been tricked, but it was too late. He would have to punish Daniel.

"It's OK," Daniel comforted the king. "My God will protect me." The king hoped he was right as the soldiers tossed Daniel into the lions' den.

King Darius didn't sleep a wink all night. At the first light of day, he rushed to the lions' den. "Daniel, did your God protect you?" he called.

"Yes, he closed the lions' mouths and kept me safe."

"Praise the God of Daniel!" the king shouted. "From now on, everyone in my kingdom should tremble in fear before Daniel's God."

BASED ON DANIEL 6

 ## Reflections From The Heart

Are you sometimes amazed at the strong faith of many of the people we read about in the Bible? Maybe some readily trusted because they actually heard God's voice or spoke with his angels. Whatever the reason, their relationships with him seem so personal.

Daniel must have cherished his communication with God—he risked his life to preserve it. He knew about the new law and probably even knew that his enemies would be watching him. But he also knew that if he gave in to them on this point, he would be asked to compromise again in the future.

Daniel's devotion to God was stronger than the threat of danger. I want that, don't you? I want God to be more important to me than anything else in the world, including any threat of persecution or danger. But you know what? I'm chicken. Yep, there, it's out in the open. I'm afraid of pain and the persecution of my loved ones. I'm a plain old egg-layin', feather-droppin' chicken. I'm not proud of it, but how do I get beyond this fear?

I think about people like Daniel or Esther, who took a stand, risked their lives, and experienced God's protection. He honored their devotion to him. Maybe the only way to develop faith and devotion like Daniel's is to take a step of faith. After we see God's protection today, we can take a bigger step tomorrow.

The challenge for today: Take the first step of developing a deep and courageous devotion to God. Begin now to trust him on a deeper level.

"God is our refuge and strength, an ever-present help in trouble."

—PSALM 46:1

Water Wings Needed

GOD HAD A JOB FOR JONAH—AN IMPOR-tant job. He wanted him to warn the people of Nineveh that they had better straighten up and live for God or else they would face major punish-ment. Jonah wasn't too happy about this opportunity to preach God's message.

"No! I'm not going to Nineveh. I hate the people there, and I know if I tell them about you and they repent of their sins, you'll forgive them. It's just the way you are. I'm not going." Jonah threw a few things into a bag and headed for the dock. "Hey, where's your ship headed?" he asked the first man he saw.

"Tarshish."

"Is that close to Nineveh?"

"No, it's the opposite direction."

"Great," Jonah said, tossing his bag on board. He settled down in the belly of the ship, believing God would never find him there. The gentle splashing of the water soon rocked Jonah to sleep.

Meanwhile, up on top, the sailors saw a storm brewing, and it looked like a big one. They pulled in the sails and did whatever they could to protect their ship. The wind blew harder and the waves grew larger. "We're in trouble! Toss things overboard; we've got to keep the ship afloat."

Jonah awoke to someone roughly shaking his shoulder. "If you've got a God, pray to him, because we're in serious trouble."

Jonah immediately realized he was the reason for their trouble. "Listen, I was trying to hide from God—obviously I didn't fool him. Throw me overboard and the storm will stop."

"No, we don't want your life on our hands," someone answered. But, Jonah insisted and eventually the desperate sailors tossed him overboard. The storm stopped immediately. As for Jonah, a gigantic fish swallowed him.

For three days and nights, while he floated around in the fish's belly, Jonah had nothing to do but think about his disobedience. "God, I'm sorry I tried to tell you what to do. Give me another chance and I'll go to Nineveh and tell them about your love." Just then the fish spit up Jonah on the shore. He pulled seaweed out of his hair and took off for Nineveh.

BASED ON JONAH 1:1–3:3

 Reflections From The Heart

Do you ever cop an attitude? Boy, Jonah did. He was sure his plan was better than God's, so he absolutely refused to obey God's instructions. Is your disobedience as blatant as Jonah's? Or are you more subtle, explaining to God (and anyone else who will listen) why you couldn't possibly do what he is suggesting?

Obedience is a word you hear a lot as a kid, and in some ways you expect it to go away as you reach adulthood. But, it doesn't. There is always something or someone to obey—bosses, policemen, laws, and of course, God. We never outgrow the need to obey.

If you sometimes have a problem with obedience, consider yourself human. We all struggle. But, we learn from the story of Jonah that we need to work on it. So, unless you like sushi and can swim really well, let go of your own agenda and do what God says.

The challenge for today: A big part of obeying is letting go of your own plans and agendas. Believe that God sees the bigger picture, and trust that his plans are best. Then, when you know what to do, do it.

"Anyone, then, who knows the good he ought to do and doesn't do it, sins." —JAMES 4:17

Blessings of Obedience

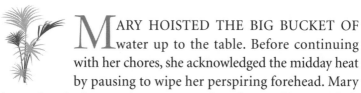MARY HOISTED THE BIG BUCKET OF water up to the table. Before continuing with her chores, she acknowledged the midday heat by pausing to wipe her perspiring forehead. Mary knew that the house was empty, so when she got that eerie feeling that someone was watching her, the hairs on the back of her neck stood on end. She turned to look at the sun-filled doorway and was surprised to see the shadow of a man there.

Slowly, he stepped into the room. "Don't be afraid, Mary. I am an angel, sent by God. I bring you good news."

Mary was so startled that she backed away from him.

"You have been chosen by God to bring his child into the world. You will give birth to a son, and you are to call him Jesus. He is God's Son and is coming to save people from their sins."

As the angel spoke, Mary realized that he was bringing her a message from God, whom she loved with all her heart. Still, it was an overwhelming message. "I, uh, I don't understand how this can be. I'm not married—I'm a virgin—so how can I have a child?"

The angel spoke gently to the frightened young girl. "The Holy Spirit will come upon you, Mary, and the shadow of almighty God will cover you. Nothing is impossible with God."

Mary's fear quietly slipped away. She whispered, "May it happen as you said; I am the Lord's servant."

BASED ON LUKE 1:26–38

Reflections From The Heart

Do you think Mary thought about those words, "I am the Lord's servant"? Did she think about how Joseph would respond to the news of her pregnancy? How about her parents or her friends? Mary's willingness to be a servant came at a cost—her reputation. It must have been sparkling clean before this, because God chose her to be the earthly mother of his son. It's safe to say that Mary's life and reputation was never the same after the angel's message. That describes a true servant's heart—no strings attached.

What kind of servant are you? Do you agree to serve, but attach a multitude of strings? Do you hold back on your servant attitude because you're afraid of what it might cost you or how it might impact your comfortable world?

Think about this—doesn't that "strings attached" attitude keep your relationship with the Master pretty superficial? Can he count on you, even when the going gets tough . . . even when it costs you something?

The challenge for today: Take a lesson from a young Jewish girl who was willing to put everything she held dear on the line to serve the Master. She knew that the outcome would be well worth her sacrifice. She was right.

"Offer yourselves to God, as those who have been brought from death to life; and offer the parts of your body to him as instruments of righteousness." —ROMANS 6:13

Perfectly Imperfect

"WHY DOES CAESAR NEED A CENSUS right now?" Joseph moaned. "Maybe Mary should stay home. I won't be gone long and her baby is due any day."

Joseph should have known better. Mary had been a social outcast since her condition became obvious. Being pregnant and unmarried was frowned upon. She and Joseph knew that her baby was the Son of God, but that wasn't something you talked about at the town well. Consequently, as Mary's tummy grew, so did the gossip. Joseph was pretty much her only friend now, so of course she would go with him to Bethlehem, rather than stay home alone.

Joseph helped Mary up on the small donkey's back and they set out on the nearly 100-mile journey to Bethlehem. "How much longer?" Mary moaned. With every step the donkey took, the baby became more active. "This baby is going to kick his way into the world."

"We're nearly there. We'll get a nice room with a soft, clean bed, and you can rest while I take care of the census." But, the streets of Bethlehem were crowded with people. The smell of sweaty, unwashed bodies and animals made Mary's stomach roll. "I'll just run and get a room. Hold on, Mary!" Joseph could see her turning green, so he dashed for the hotel. He was back too soon. "They don't have any rooms left. The whole town is full because of the census. The innkeeper will let us stay in the stable, because you're pregnant. I'm so sorry, Mary."

At the moment, Mary didn't care. "Just get me off this donkey," she whispered through gritted teeth. In the stable, Joseph piled some straw together for Mary to lie on. She fell right to sleep, so he tended to the donkey, trying to think of their options. There weren't any. He was yanked back to reality when Mary cried, "The baby is coming. I don't want to have my baby in a dirty stable. Please, Joseph, do something!"

But there was nothing he could do, until it was time to pull the baby from her body. "A boy. Mary, it's a boy, just as the angel said."

Mary cradled the little one in her arms and whispered, "Hello, sweet one. Your name is Jesus."

BASED ON LUKE 2:1–7

 Reflections From The Heart

Have you ever seen someone famous? Were you able to sit down and talk with the celebrity? Did you swap childhood stories? Did this world-renowned person stay in your home? You ended up being best friends, right?

Usually the rich and famous associate with the rich and famous. They tend to travel in the same circles, rarely associating with us common folk. If you happened to see a celebrity in a hotel lobby or airport terminal, the crowd probably parted so he could be escorted through. No one could get close to him.

In contrast, Jesus was born to common parents instead of royalty because he came for all people. Think about that—he is as approachable to a poor, single mom as he is to a president or king, and everyone in between. It was important that the Savior be approachable, so people could relate to him.

As the Savior's representative in this world, are you approachable? Do people feel that they can talk to you? Do you show the heart of Jesus by the way you relate to others? Do you prefer the well-dressed, educated people of society, or are you taking the Savior, born in a stable, to the outcast and needy, too?

The challenge for today: Reach outside your comfort zone and share Christ's love with all those who need to know about it.

"For God so loved the world that he gave his one and only Son, that whoever believes in him shall not perish but have eternal life."
—JOHN 3:16

Keep On Keeping On

MARY, JOSEPH, AND SEVERAL OF THEIR friends and relatives were walking back home after celebrating Passover in Jerusalem. "I haven't seen Jesus all day, have you?" asked Mary. Joseph wasn't worried. Twelve-year-old Jesus was more than likely with some of his friends. The boys liked to walk together and play games to pass the time.

"No, I haven't. Maybe I'll walk ahead and see who he's with," Joseph answered. But Jesus wasn't with any of his friends. None of them had seen him all day. They thought he was with his mom and dad. "Mary, no one has seen him. Did we leave him in Jerusalem?" Joseph's heart raced.

Mary and Joseph ran back to Jerusalem. By the time they reached the city, Mary's side ached, but fear pushed her on. "He's only twelve; what will happen to him?" They ran to the inn where they had stayed, but Jesus wasn't there. For three days Mary and Joseph searched, stopping people on the street to ask if they had seen the young boy. No one had.

Tears rolled down Mary's cheeks as she choked out her fear. "What if we never see him again? Joseph, what are we going to do?" Before Joseph could answer, a group of people passed by, talking excitedly among themselves about a young boy in the temple who was teaching the teachers. A light went on in Mary's heart—it had to be Jesus. They rushed to the temple and, sure enough, there was Jesus, surrounded by the old teachers. He was answering their questions and teaching them things about God.

"We've been looking everywhere for you," Mary said. "Why did you do this?"

Jesus was surprised by her question, "Didn't you know that I would be in my Father's house?" But, he went home with Mary and Joseph. Mary couldn't stop touching his shoulder or brushing back his hair. "He's safe, he's really safe," her heart sang.

BASED ON LUKE 2:41–52

 Reflections From The Heart

OK, be honest. At times don't you wonder what on earth God is doing . . . or if he's doing anything at all? Do you wonder if he even sees what's going on down here on earth?

Well, rest easy. God knows what he's doing. Even as a child, Jesus understood who he was and what he had come to earth to do. He knew things about God that the older, more experienced (and supposedly wiser) teachers didn't know, and he recognized that it was his job to share those insights. He even thought that Mary and Joseph should have realized right away where he was and what he was doing.

But they didn't. Imagine their panic as they realized that they had lost Jesus—the Son of God. The almighty God had entrusted them with his Son and they lost him! You can bet that they took off running to Jerusalem, and that they searched every nook and cranny, every place they had stayed, every place they had gone, and anything that might have looked appealing to a twelve-year-old boy. They didn't give up until they found him. They persevered in searching for Jesus, their son . . . their Savior.

The challenge for today: Whether or not you understand what God is doing, seek him diligently. Persevere in looking for Jesus in every aspect of life. Then, trust him and learn from him as he teaches you about himself.

"You will find him if you look for him with all your heart and with all your soul." —DEUTERONOMY 4:29

Preparing the Way

SOME PEOPLE DIDN'T KNOW WHAT TO make of John the Baptist. He was passionate about his work, but he was more than a little strange. He lived alone in the wilderness, he wore clothing made from camel's hair, and he ate bugs and honey— you would not want to bring this guy home for dinner. Still, the message he so passionately preached grabbed people's hearts and changed their lives.

"Stop sinning! Repent and give your hearts to God!" The strange-looking man certainly got people's attention as he wandered from town to town preaching. "Stop thinking only of yourselves. If you have two coats and you see a man with none, give him one of yours. If you have food and a neighbor has none, share what you have."

His message made sense. After individuals grasped John's words and let them sink into their hearts, he led them into the Jordan River and baptized them.

"We've been waiting hundreds of years for the Messiah to come. Perhaps this man is the Messiah," someone observed.

Excited converts went to John and asked him if he was the one for whom they had been waiting.

"No, I'm only preparing you for the one to come after me," John said firmly. "I baptize with water, but he will baptize you with the Holy Spirit. I assure you that I'm not even worthy to untie his shoes. Be ready for him."

BASED ON LUKE 3

Reflections From The Heart

John the Baptist knew that his job was to get people ready to receive Jesus or at least to hear Jesus' message, so that's what he did. He didn't try to draw attention away from the Messiah and toward himself.

When you have a job to do, do it, even if you aren't the star. A team of any kind, be it a sports team or a musical ensemble that doesn't work together is destined to fail. On a healthy team, each member supports the others as they strive toward a common goal. That's a healthier scenario than a team that revolves around a super star. Are you comfortable in a supporting role?

Scripture tells us that, as believers, we are part of a body—the body of Christ. We need to accept our role in that body. What would happen to our physical body if one part went on strike? For example, do the elbows typically get much attention? No . . . but just try spending a day without bending your arms.

John the Baptist spent his life getting people ready for the main event—the Messiah. He knew his job and he did it well.

The challenge for today: Know your job and do it well. If you are a supporting player in a ministry, support to the very best of your ability.

"Now you are the body of Christ, and each one of you is a part of it."
—1 CORINTHIANS 12:27

Temptation Is Nothing New

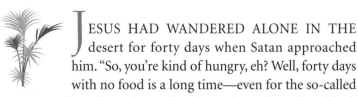

JESUS HAD WANDERED ALONE IN THE desert for forty days when Satan approached him. "So, you're kind of hungry, eh? Well, forty days with no food is a long time—even for the so-called Son of God." Lucifer spoke softly to Jesus' heart. "Here's an idea," he whispered. "If you are really the Son of God, why don't you just tell those stones over there to turn into bread. You can eat all you want."

Exhaustion, hunger, and loneliness put Jesus in the weakest of human conditions, but not weak enough to fall prey to Satan's suggestion. "The Scriptures say that man does not live by bread alone," he answered.

Satan wasn't finished with him yet. Taking Jesus to the top of a mountain, he waved his hand over the countryside. "All the kingdoms of this world belong to me. Wouldn't you enjoy ruling them . . . being their king? That position is mine to bestow on whomever I choose. I'll give it to you, Jesus; all you have to do is worship me. That's not asking so much, is it, hmmm?"

"It is written, 'Worship the Lord your God and serve him only,'" Jesus responded, once again quoting from the Scriptures.

Now Satan was frustrated. He whisked Jesus to the highest point of the temple in Jerusalem. "I know the Scriptures, too. If you are truly the Son of God, you can throw yourself down from here, because your precious Scriptures say, 'He will command his angels concerning you to guard you carefully; they will lift you up in their hands, so that you will not strike your foot against a stone.'"

Jesus had had enough. "The Scriptures say, 'Do not test the Lord your God!'" Satan snorted as he left. He wasn't finished with Jesus. He would be back.

BASED ON LUKE 4:1–13

 ## Reflections From The Heart

When you're tempted, don't go whining to Jesus that he doesn't know what you're going through. He does. Satan tested Jesus in the three categories into which sin generally falls: self-gratification, self-promotion, and self-preservation.

Look at the first one. "What? You're hungry? Oh poor Jesus. Well, why don't you just turn these stones into bread and have lunch?" Jesus' mouth probably watered, but he chose obedience over self-gratification. When you want to justify your sins by saying, "I deserve this," "It makes me feel better," or "I've had a really bad day," remember that Jesus has been there and he didn't give in.

The second category, self-promotion, is a struggle, too. We all want to feel important and valuable to those around us. It's nice to be in charge. But, Jesus knew that reaching that position in the wrong way wasn't worth it.

Self-preservation is certainly near and dear to most people's hearts. We want to save our own skin, and usually we'll do whatever it takes. But the Son of God didn't bite on Satan's temptation here, either. Jesus had nothing to prove—he knew who was in charge. That's why he never caved in to temptation.

The challenge for today: Be prepared. Temptation will come, it's just a matter of when and what form it will take. Know the Scriptures, so you can fight back. Know your boundaries of right and wrong—then stick to them. Pray continually for God's help and strength in facing temptation.

"God is faithful; he will not let you be tempted beyond what you can bear." —1 CORINTHIANS 10:13

The Little Things Matter

I love weddings, Mary thought as she fixed her hair and put on her best dress. She enjoyed watching the starry-eyed couple and visiting with the family and friends she didn't get to see often.

The service was just as lovely as Mary imagined, and the party afterward was filled with laughter and joy. A couple of hours into the reception, however, Mary heard the panic-stricken host say, "How can we be out of wine? The party is just starting. What am I going to do?"

His problem struck a chord with Mary, so she shared it with her son. "Jesus, our friend ran out of wine, and the party is just starting. This will disgrace him in front of his family and friends."

"Mother, it's not time for me to do miracles yet," Jesus replied. Mary gave him the look that only a mother can give. Then she said to some servants nearby, "Do whatever this man tells you to do." She stood aside expectantly.

Jesus looked around at the people having so much fun. He saw the happy bride and groom and the anxious host. He raised his face to heaven and closed his eyes for a moment. Then he directed the servants, "Fill those six large jars with water." After, they did, Jesus said, "Now, draw some out and take it to the host of the party."

A hopeful smile tugged at Mary's lips as she watched. She almost laughed out loud when the host sipped from the spoon and his eyes grew as big as saucers. He ran to the bridegroom and cried, "This is the best wine I've ever tasted! Most people serve the best wine first and the second-rate stuff later. You saved the best for last."

BASED ON JOHN 2:1–11

 Reflections From The Heart

Do you ever think that Jesus isn't concerned with the everyday things of life? Does it seem like a waste of his valuable time for you to talk to him about your day in and day out concerns? Do you take only the big stuff to him and handle the little things yourself?

This story of Jesus' first miracle shows that he does care about our everyday concerns. Running out of wine at the wedding party was certainly not a life or death matter, though it may have been embarrassing to the host. But, Jesus cared enough to make this his first public miracle. The need was there; he cared; he acted.

Jesus knows what you deal with every day and that those things can get you down. When the computer crashes just before

THE LITTLE THINGS MATTER

you save a big document, your pipes freeze and flood your home, or the car breaks down, he cares. God's compassion and power are not limited to earth-shaking, life or death problems. He knows that normal life presents problems every day.

What have you been trying to handle on your own? Have you thought that you don't need God's help on that issue, or that you shouldn't bother him with such a piddling little thing? Remember, he cared about a wedding reception and the beverage of the day.

The challenge for today: Trust him enough to try him with daily life. He cares.

"Trust in the LORD *and do good."* —PSALM 37:3

Someone You
Should Know

JESUS AND HIS DISCIPLES HAD BEEN WALK-
ing all day. He was hot, tired, and thirsty when he
sat down beside a well to rest. While his friends went
into town to buy some food a woman approached
the well to draw water.

"Could I have some water?" Jesus asked her. His request wasn't
unusual—the woman had been asked the same thing hundreds
of times. But, never by a Jew.

"Well, my, my . . . a high and mighty Jew stoops to ask a lowly
Samaritan woman for a drink?"

Jesus was tired and hungry, but he gently responded, "If you
knew who is asking you for a drink, you would be asking me for
living water."

"Right," she snarled. "You have no bucket to draw water.
Where are you going to get this 'living water'?"

"Everyone who drinks of this water will get thirsty again. But, those who drink the water I offer will never again thirst," Jesus spoke softly. His words cut to her heart.

"Great, give me some," she said, fighting the odd feeling swimming around in her heart. "Give me your water and I won't have to come to this well anymore."

"Go get your husband."

Jesus' words caught her off guard. "Uhh, I'm not married," she finally blurted out.

"Yes, but you've had five husbands . . . and you're not married to the man you're living with now."

"What you are some—kind of Jewish prophet?" the woman quickly regained her attitude. "Our ancestors have always worshiped on this mountain, but you Jews say we have to worship in some temple in Jerusalem."

"God loves you and he wants your worship—wherever it comes."

"Aah, I don't know." She tossed up her hands in exasperation. "I don't understand all this. Maybe when the Messiah comes it will all make sense." She started to walk away.

"I am the Messiah."

His words sank into her heart, and she slowly realized he was telling the truth. Water splashed from her jar as she ran back to town shouting, "I met the Messiah!" Grabbing people by the arm, she pulled them toward the well. "Come with me. I want you to meet him, too!" Many people believed in Jesus that day because the woman shared the good news with everyone she met.

BASED ON JOHN 4:1–42

Reflections From The Heart

Have you ever felt an urgency and excitement to tell someone your news? Perhaps when you got a big promotion at work, or when you got engaged, or your first child was born? Those news items simply must be shared!

When the woman at the well realized she was talking to the Messiah, she wanted to share him with others—even people she didn't know. She nearly dragged people out to the well to meet him.

Have you ever had the joy of leading someone to Christ? Is the news of his love still as thrilling to you as when you were a newborn Christian? Remember that almost uncontainable excitement? Christ's love is the best news in the world! Why are we sometimes so unenthusiastic about sharing it? Where's our joy?

Perhaps, unlike the woman at the well, we think too much about how people will respond to our witness. We don't want our peers to perceive us as fanatics, and we don't want our friends to tease us or make fun of us. The woman at the well had lived a hard life and perhaps wasn't so well thought of by the nice people in town. Still, after meeting Jesus, she simply exploded with joy, and she couldn't keep it inside. She apparently didn't even think about who she was bringing to Jesus; she grabbed anyone who would listen.

The challenge for today: Recapture the joy of a new Christian heart. Combine that with the knowledge that people who don't know Christ are lost for a Christless eternity. Share the news of God's love urgently and often.

"For the wages of sin is death, but the gift of God is eternal life in Christ Jesus our Lord." —ROMANS 6:23

Picnic Party

"SON, IT'S OK IF YOU GO LISTEN TO JESUS teach, but let me pack you a lunch first."

"Mama, I don't have time. My friends are waiting. Anyway, I had a big breakfast." Her son backed toward the door.

"It will take me thirty seconds to wrap up some fish and bread." The boy wasn't happy about it, but he waited, then tucked the small package under his coat. His friends would call him a baby or a Mama's boy if they saw it.

Thousands of people had gathered to hear Jesus teach. The boy and his friends picked their way through the crowd and sat down near the front. Jesus began teaching, and everyone listened quietly for hours. The only other sound was the occasional chirp of a bird. When the sun was sinking low in the sky, one of Jesus' friends slipped up to him and whispered, "It's getting late. Why don't you send the people into town to get food?"

The young boy's heart sank. He was enjoying listening to Jesus so much that he didn't want the day to end. But then Jesus answered his friend, "No, you give the people food."

"Where are we going to get enough food to feed all these people? It would take a year's wages to buy enough."

"You can have my lunch." The boy held out the little bit of food that he had tucked inside his coat. He was embarrassed when the man spouted something about how that little crumb of a lunch couldn't help with all these people.

Yet, to the boy's amazement, Jesus took the bag, lifted the food to the sky, and thanked God for it. Then he broke the five loaves of bread and two fish into pieces. When the disciples instructed people to sit down in groups of fifty, the boy realized he had been holding his breath. Jesus' friends passed the food out to the people. More than five thousand people had all they wanted to eat—and twelve baskets of food were left over. And it all came from the young boy's lunch. Wiping crumbs from his face, the boy smiled at Jesus, who smiled right back. They had just shared in a miracle.

BASED ON JOHN 6:1–13

 Reflections From The Heart

What an exciting experience for this little boy! His generous act of sharing allowed him to participate in an awesome miracle. He must have realized that his little lunch wouldn't make a dent in feeding the big crowd, but that wasn't his concern. He simply gave what he had and let Jesus handle the rest.

Did you ever think, "Well, how could my measly five-dollar gift help missions? It takes millions of dollars to get a ministry up and running." What a great . . . excuse. Yeah, excuse. We each must answer for our own stewardship, our willingness to give what we have. God can take a thousand five-dollar gifts and use them to do something significant, but if individuals don't do their part, nothing gets done.

Sometimes we forget that our God can take a little gift, given from a sincere heart, and use it in a big way. Certainly this applies to the tithes and offerings given to his work, but he also can use a talent or an interest that we may think is nothing special. When it's given to him, he can use it to touch lives and change hearts. Jesus encouraged us to care for others. He even said that feeding the hungry, clothing the naked, and befriending the friendless was a way of serving and honoring him (Matthew 25:31–46).

The challenge for today: Don't worry about what difference your little gift can make. Give your money or share your talents and let God decide how to use them. Your willing and generous spirit may allow you to share in a miracle, too!

"God is not unjust; he will not forget your work and the love you have shown him as you have helped his people and continue to help them." —HEBREWS 6:10

Check Your Priorities

A TRICKLE OF SWEAT SLID DOWN MARTHA'S forehead as she kneaded the bread dough. Tossing it into a bowl, she peeked around the corner. Her sister, Mary, hummed as she strolled around the table, arranging silverware. *All afternoon just to set the table,* Martha sighed. Turning to her to-do list, Martha scratched through two more chores. Since she had heard Jesus was coming, Martha had barely sat down. She had washed curtains, dusted furniture, scrubbed floors, even cleaned closets. Everything had to be perfect. She simply couldn't settle for less.

All her life Martha had been a doer. She could handle a job from beginning to end. Truthfully, though, Mary was the more popular of the sisters. She loved talking with people, and neighbors often stopped by just to chat with her. When they needed a job done, however, people went straight to Martha.

Suddenly there was a knock at the door. "He's here! Martha! Jesus is here!" Silverware clanked to the floor as Mary ran to the door. Martha dried her hands on her apron and ran to hug Jesus. Then Mary led him to a comfortable chair, and she settled down on a nearby footstool. Martha chatted for a few minutes, before her heart pulled her back to the kitchen. As she chopped vegetables, Martha could hear Mary and Jesus laughing. Every few minutes she peeked out, hoping that Mary was coming to help with the last-minute preparations. She wasn't.

It wouldn't hurt Mary to help me finish dinner, Martha fretted. *After all, I've done nearly everything.* The more Martha thought about it, the more frustrated she got. Soon she was slamming pots onto the counter and throwing pans into the oven. *If Mary would get in here and help me, then maybe I could sit down and talk to Jesus, too!*

A few minutes later, Mary's delighted laughter erupted again. That did it! Martha threw down the dishtowel and stomped into the other room. "Hey, has anyone noticed that I'm doing all the work here? Jesus, tell her to get up and help me! Then I'll have time to talk with you, too." Mary was genuinely startled at her sister's outburst, but Jesus smiled gently before speaking.

"Martha, dear, dear Martha. You work so hard. I appreciate your clean house and dinner smells wonderful. But you're missing out on what really counts. Mary understands that spending time with me is more important than a fancy dinner. To tell the truth, I would rather have bread and cheese, and time to talk with you. Sit down, Martha. Tell me how you're doing."

BASED ON LUKE 10:38–42

Reflections From The Heart

Martha believed she was doing the right thing, certainly nothing is wrong with preparing a wonderful dinner and serving it in a clean house. Martha's problem was her priorities—she was focusing on her service more than on whom she was serving. It is a subtle shift, and it can happen so slowly.

Are you ever caught in a struggle to keep your daily priorities straight? Good, that means you're normal (small comfort, huh?). It's so easy to start each day determined to keep God first, family second, and everything else a distant third. But, before the day is very old, those third place items creep (or sometimes fly) into first place. It's an age-old story—the squeaky wheel gets the oil, and the urgent needs always squeak more loudly than the important ones.

This story is a gentle reminder to check your priorities—daily. What's really more important? Quiet time with God or writing a report for work? Playing with your children or chasing dust bunnies under the bed? Having coffee with a friend who is hurting or waxing the kitchen floor?

Keeping your busy life in line and your priorities in focus is not something you can muscle your way through—you need help. Determining where to spend your time and energy is an event-by-event decision. The wisdom to make each choice comes from being close to God. We're promised as we depend on him, God will renew our strength (Isaiah 40:29–31).

The challenge for today: Learn a lesson from Martha. Keep close to God and ask for his help to keep your priorities straight. Don't let the urgent push aside the important. This takes a minute-by-minute effort and conscious decisions, and it requires calling on God for wisdom and strength. Don't get discouraged if some days you slide back into flip-flopped priorities. It happens. Just confess, ask his help, and start again.

"Love the Lord your God with all your heart and with all your soul and with all your mind and with all your strength. . . . Love your neighbor as yourself." —MARK 12:30–31

I Don't Care What Others Think

THE WOMAN HAD MET JESUS ONCE before, and he had chased away the demons that haunted her mind and heart. Since then, her life was changed and she would be forever thankful. Now she stood outside Simon's house, hoping to see Jesus as a group of men went in for dinner. *I just want to see him. I won't bother anyone,* the woman thought.

She did catch a quick glimpse of Jesus as the men went inside. She knew she wasn't welcome in the house because her lifestyle wasn't socially acceptable. She slipped across the yard to peek in a window. The men were reclining around a table, talking and eating. Jesus was right in the middle.

Suddenly, she was overcome with emotion. Racing home, she yanked open a cupboard and grabbed a beautiful alabaster jar filled with perfume—the most valuable thing she owned. Hurrying back to Simon's, she hesitated at the door, and took a deep breath before entering.

All conversations stopped . . . every eye was on her. She knelt at Jesus' feet, tears rolling down her face onto his feet. Loosing her long hair, she gently wiped away those tears. Then, breaking open the jar, she poured the perfume on Jesus' feet. She was vaguely aware of whispered comments. "Why is he letting that sinful woman touch him?" "Doesn't he know what kind of person she is?" Jesus stopped the criticisms and lifted her to her feet. Once again, her heart overflowed with love for him.

BASED ON LUKE 7:36–50

 ## Reflections From The Heart

This lady was pretty gutsy, wasn't she? She knew she wasn't welcome in Simon's home. After all, she had two strikes against her—she was female and a prostitute. But her love for Jesus and her gratitude to him were more powerful than her fear of the men's insults. Peer pressure apparently didn't mean much to her. The love she felt for Jesus was so overwhelming that everything else fell into the shadows.

Whew! This could be convicting. Do you ever sugarcoat your devotion to God so that it's acceptable to your coworkers, family, or friends? No one wants to look like some kind of weirdo. Do you smooth over your Christian standards, water them down, to make life more comfortable for those around you?

Jesus said that believers are the salt in this world—a light on a dark hill (Matthew 5:13–15). Our love for God and others should make us conspicuous. Otherwise how will people know what life with God is like or even what he is like? If our lives look like everyone else's, then what makes Christianity appealing?

The challenge for today: Take a risk. Moving forward in life always involves a risk. Stop caring so much about what other people think. Concentrate on what God thinks.

"Be on your guard; stand firm in the faith; be men of courage; be strong. Do everything in love." —1 CORINTHIANS 16:13–14

Nothing to Lose

TWELVE YEARS. DOCTOR AFTER DOCTOR, yet nothing helped. She was still as sick as ever. The poor woman was at the end of her rope, physically and emotionally. Her finances were exhausted, and she was lonely. This unexplained bleeding made her unclean, and everyone she loved—family, friends—had taken a step back from her.

Then, one day she heard that the teacher from Nazareth was coming through town. People said he healed those who were blind or lame. Some said he freed people whose very souls had been taken over by demons. If the stories were all true, he even brought dead people back to life. So what if people made fun of her for trying? So what if some thought she was crazy? It might be her last chance to restore some normalcy to her life. *What do I have to lose?*

The woman followed the crowd surrounding Jesus as he walked down the street. There were so many people that no one even noticed her. She stayed on the fringe, listening to people talk, and working up her courage. Finally, adrenaline surging, she dived forward and grabbed the hem of his robe. Immediately, she felt . . . something. A shocked "Oooohhhhh!" escaped from her lips before she slapped a hand over her mouth. She fell to the back of the crowd, trying to understand what had just happened.

Jesus stopped so suddenly that people behind him bumped into each other.

"Who touched me?" he asked.

His followers couldn't believe the question. Who touched him? Hundreds of people were in the crowd walking with him. People must have brushed against him a dozen times a minute—was he serious?

"Who touched me?" he asked again.

The woman wanted to turn and run. She took a step away. But, she couldn't go. Something had happened when she touched his robe, and she couldn't ignore it.

"I did. I touched your robe," she said softly. Stepping forward she whispered, "I've been sick so long and . . . I thought, if I could just touch your robe, I'd be well. When I did touch you, I felt something." She could barely get the next words out. "I think I'm well."

People in the crowd gasped, but he understood. He stepped forward and brushed his hand against her cheek. "Go in peace, your faith has made you well."

BASED ON MARK 5:25–34

 Reflections From The Heart

Have you ever been at the end of your rope? The kids have whined or fought for days, your husband is out of town, your best friend moved away, a pipe in the bathroom breaks, turning the downstairs family room into a shower, and . . . once again, you've fallen off your diet. Or maybe your life looks even darker. Your husband left, and he's not coming back, or you're struggling with a serious illness. We've all experienced times when our resources are exhausted and we've nowhere to turn . . . except to Jesus.

That's where this woman was. So she stepped out with take-a-chance-nothing-to-lose faith. She took a risk, regardless of what other people might think, regardless of being put on display in front of the crowd. What incredible courage! And she was rewarded.

Sometimes our view of God limits his freedom to work in our lives. We put God in a box and smugly say, "God does things this way, but he doesn't do things that way." A. W. Tozer in *The Knowledge of the Holy* suggests that everything we do—everything we say—every choice we make is a theological decision. That means our decisions, our prayers, our attitudes show our opinion of who God is, even if we're not thinking about him at the moment. So I ask you, how big is your God?

This woman's story reminds us to break down the walls of the box we comfortably keep God in and to expand our view of what he can do. Her example encourages us to pray for the seemingly impossible, trust for the incredible, and love to the maximum. We, too, can step out in faith, which is the confident assurance that what we hope for is going to happen, no matter how incredible or impossible it may seem.

The challenge for today: Ask God to grow in you a faith so strong that you believe that a fingertip reaching and stretching to touch the hem of Jesus' robe can heal a twelve-year illness. Then, be courageous; take the first step. Trust completely and prepare to be amazed at what God will do.

"Now faith is being sure of what we hope for and certain of what we do not see." —HEBREWS 11:1

With Friends Like These . . .

THE FOUR MEN FELT BAD FOR THEIR PAR-
alyzed friend. They often stopped by to cheer
him up and share news of what was happening around
town. But they always wished they could do more.

"Hey, I heard that Jesus is in town. People say he can heal sick
people. Maybe he would help our friend," said one of them.

"Yeah, maybe, but how do we get him to Jesus?" asked
another.

"I don't know. There has to be a way!" The four friends huddled together and came up with a gutsy idea. Soon they were back
at their friend's house, dragging a makeshift cot and a long piece
of rope. "Smooth your hair and spit shine your toes—you're
going on a trip," they announced to their friend.

The surprised man was speechless when his friends lifted him
onto the cot and carried him through Capernaum. "This is the

place," one friend said, stopping at a small crowded house where people spilled out the doorways and windows. "Let us through," he called. No one moved. "Come on, we just want to get our friend to Jesus." Still, no one budged.

"We need Plan B," he called to his friends. They huddled together once again. "That's it!" the man shouted. They quickly carried their friend up the outside stairs and began digging a hole in the roof. They heard shouts from the room below as grass, dirt, and pieces of tile fell on the men sitting there. Nevertheless, the four determined men kept digging and finally had a hole large enough to lower their paralyzed friend down in front of Jesus. He saw the faith and hope in their eyes, and Jesus' heart was touched. So, he turned to the sick man and healed him. You know there was a friend-hugging celebration in his house that night!

BASED ON MARK 2:1–5

 ## Reflections From The Heart

What cool friends! They went out of their way to help a friend in need. They left their family, jobs, and their own agendas to reach out to him. What incredible faith, too. They went to all the work of carrying the man across town, trying to get through the crowd of people around the front door, coming up with Plan B, and risking the anger of the homeowner and the cost of repairing his home, all because they believed Jesus could make a difference to their friend.

Has a friend ever gone out of her way to help you? How did you feel about her after that? How did you feel about helping others yourself? Were you more willing to reach out?

Helping others usually involves a sacrifice of some kind. Time is the big one—time away from work, family, friends, and your own needs. Helping someone almost always takes longer than you planned, and you can't just stop in the middle.

Sometimes you also sacrifice your reputation. The people who saw the four friends carrying the sick man may have initially thought the men were kind and generous, but when they saw them ripping up someone's roof, they probably thought the guys were crazy.

Helping someone also requires hard work. Think about the four men in the story. They had to carry their friend across town and up the stairs to the roof of the house. Then they dug a hole large enough to lower the man through. None of this was easy. In fact, as their plans for helping the man changed, the job got more involved than they had bargained for, but they didn't stop.

Do you go out of your way to help others? Do you believe that bringing them before the Lord will make a difference in their lives? Can Jesus help them? Will he?

The challenge for today: Learn from these four friends. Invest time, risk your reputation, and work hard to help others. Do what you physically can and also bring your friends before the Lord in prayer.

"Each one should use whatever gift he has received to serve others, faithfully administering God's grace in its various forms."

—1 PETER 4:10

No Holds Barred

THE SHRIVELED LITTLE WOMAN STOOD behind a pillar in the temple. Her clothes were clean, but ragged. Her stomach growled loudly and she clamped her hand over it, willing her body to silence. She would never want to call attention to herself or disturb the worshipful atmosphere of the temple.

She watched as the people in line put their money in the offering box. *I love this,* she thought, *all these people gathered in God's house, giving their offerings to him—worshipping him. I praise you, God, for all you have given me!* If anyone had heard the woman's thoughts, they would have assumed she had lost her mind. Her husband was dead, and she barely had two coins to rub together. She hardly even knew where her next meal was coming from. What reason did she have to praise God?

The average observer didn't know that, even though the woman was alone in the world, she wasn't alone in her heart. She loved God completely. Every day she came to the temple to worship and praise him and to give an offering, when she had anything to give. Today the woman stepped into the line of people waiting to give. She prayed as she waited for her turn.

In front of her, a man dressed in fine purple robes held a big bag of coins. He made quite a show of taking a few coins out of the bag. When he stepped up to the offering box, he prayed loudly, announcing how fortunate God was to have a servant like him. After every few words, he glanced around to make sure everyone in the temple was watching him. Apparently he thought people should congratulate God that such an important man was giving an offering.

Next, the old woman shyly stepped up to the box and slipped two coins into the slot. Added together the coins were barely worth a penny . . . but it was all she had. She bowed her head and silently prayed that the money would be used to help those who were less fortunate than her.

Her prayer was interrupted by the rich man's loud voice, "Ha! What a worthless offering. Those two coins will do nothing— they're not even worth the space they take up in the box." Soon others joined the arrogant man in mocking her small gift.

The woman kept her eyes down as she moved away from the crowd. When she did look up, she saw Jesus watching her from across the room. He knew that this woman's heart belonged to God. She had just given everything she had to God's work—not extra money or leftover money, but everything. She saw the approval in Jesus' eyes and once again her heart sang with praise to God.

BASED ON MARK 12:41–44

Reflections From The Heart

This story is so convicting. Oh sure, I give to God's work. I give my money, my time, and my energy. But, is my giving sacrificial? No, I tithe from my earnings. I may even give a little extra when I have it, but I have never given everything I have. After all, I have to think of my needs and do my part to help take care of my family. I give time and energy to his work, but I make sure I have time left for me. And if that *me* time gets a little crowded, you can bet I complain about it—loudly.

We can learn two lessons from this woman. First, she seemed to truly worship God by her giving. She lived her life by faith. She was willing to give until it hurt—give all that she had. She wasn't giving the excess of her riches, or the leftover money. She dug deep in her pocket and pulled out a handful of lint and two small coins. Brushing away the lint, she dropped the coins in the box.

Second, she trusted God to take care of her everyday needs. She didn't hold on to her coins to ensure she would have food for her next meal. She gave them, out of a heart full of love for God, and she left her next meal to be his worry. I'm sure he handled it.

Compare this woman to the rich man who gave his offering before her. He wanted everyone to know how important he was, to see how much money he gave. Once he had everyone's attention, he wanted them to hear his prayer and see how generous his offering was. He was pretty impressed with himself, and apparently he thought that God, as well as the other people in the temple, should be impressed with him, too. He wasn't giving from a heart filled with love for God and others; he was giving because it made him look good.

This poor woman prayed quietly. She worshipped God as she gave, and she gave all she had . . . no holds barred. Jesus summed it up (doesn't he always?). He pointed out that she gave more than all the others because they gave out of their wealth, but she gave out of her poverty.

The challenge for today: Learn from this generous woman's example.

"Do nothing out of selfish ambition or vain conceit, but in humility consider others better than yourselves." —PHILIPPIANS 2:3

Two Simple Words

VICTIMS OF LEPROSY, A SKIN-EATING DIS-ease, were shunned—forced to live together in a leper colony outside of town. It was a lonely life. "I miss my family," cried one man. "It's been four years since I've been able to hug my kids or kiss my wife. I doubt if my youngest girl even remembers me. This disease is probably going to kill me, and I'm at the point of wishing that would happen sooner rather than later."

"I know what you mean. This isn't living . . . it's existing and waiting to die," another man said quietly.

"Everybody inside! People are coming down the road!" cried one of the lepers, warning the others to hide.

"Hey, it's that teacher from Nazareth—Jesus. He can heal sick people and even bring the dead back to life."

That gave some of the lepers an idea. Ten men boldly stepped forward and called out, "Jesus! Have mercy on us. Please heal us!"

The crowd of people around Jesus stepped back in disgust. "Get away from us!" But, Jesus looked at the men with compassion.

"Go show yourselves to the priest," he told the men.

Obediently, the men ran toward the temple in town. As they were going, one man noticed his skin beginning to clear. "I'm healed! He did it!" he cried. Someone else shouted, "I can't wait to see my family!" Nine of the men ran to town as fast as their newly healed legs would carry them.

The tenth man stopped and looked at his hands. The white leprosy spots were gone. His skin was pink and healthy. Tears flowing down his cheeks, he went back to Jesus. Looking into his gentle eyes, he whispered, "Thank you."

Jesus smiled at him, then looked around expectantly. "Where are the others? Didn't I heal ten men?" He was sad that the others hadn't taken time to thank him.

BASED ON LUKE 17:11–19

Reflections From The Heart

Saying thanks. It takes such a small amount of time and effort, but it means so much. Whether or not you thank others speaks volumes regarding how you feel about what they did for you. These ten men apparently had been sick with leprosy for quite some time, and of course they missed their families and any semblance of normal life. That even emphasizes more the value and importance of what Jesus did for them. By healing them, Jesus gave them back their lives. Wouldn't you think that something that big would merit a "thank you," even if they had to delay seeing their loved ones for a few more minutes? It must have been important to Jesus, because he noticed that nine of the men didn't come to thank him.

Do you remember to thank God for what he does? You probably do for the big things. What about the things God does for you every single day, the things you may be taking for granted or expecting him to do. Doesn't he deserve thanks for those things, too?

Saying thanks means you have noticed what was done for you and that you acknowledge the effort it took to do it. Saying thanks shows you appreciate the act and the person who performed it.

Have you ever gone out of your way to do something for others, and they simply walked away after receiving your gift, as if they deserved your effort? You probably felt little motivation to do anything for them again. God isn't as petty as we are (thank goodness), but based on this story of the ten lepers, we know that he appreciates our gratitude.

The challenge for today: Thank him for one new thing every single day.

"Give thanks to the LORD, call on his name; make known among the nations what he has done." —1 CHRONICLES 16:8

A Father's Love

"I GOTTA GET OUT OF HERE! IT'S BAD enough that Dad wasted his life on this lousy farm. I'm not gonna be a hayseed, too!" the young boy shouted.

"We've got work to do," his older brother snarled. "Save your complaining for your own time."

That night the boy approached his dad with an idea. "When you die, I'll inherit a big share of your money. How about giving it to me now, so I can go live the life I want?" The father was saddened by his son's attitude, but he granted his request.

The father watched his son sprint away to a life that he had no idea how to manage. The boy hit the city running, money rolled through his fingers like water, and he was soon surrounded by those willing to help him spend it. Nights were filled with parties and laughter.

One day the boy awoke to the reality that his money was gone. Just as quickly, his new friends were gone—they had moved on to the next big spender. He was alone, no place to live, nothing to eat. Finally, he got so hungry that he had no choice but to get a job, and the only work he could find was slopping pigs. *I've blown it big time. I couldn't wait to get away from farm life, but now look at me. I wish I could go home. Maybe I could just ask Dad to hire me as a worker. I don't deserve to be called his son anymore.*

All the way home he rehearsed the speech he would give his dad. He was still quite a ways from the farm when he saw someone running toward him, waving and shouting. As the person got closer he realized it was his father.

"My son is home!" he shouted.

The boy tried to give his speech, but he couldn't get a word in edgewise.

"My son is home! Kill the fattest calf! We're going to party all night!"

BASED ON LUKE 15:11–32

 ## Reflections From The Heart

What a dad! Complete, total, unreserved forgiveness. No questions asked—just immediate wide open arms. That boy must have been so astonished . . . and grateful. Do you think he was repentant and appreciative of his dad? Do you think this experience made him more forgiving of others?

This story is a picture of God's total forgiveness. We can be rebellious and arrogant, making bad choices, and even ambivalent toward him, but when we start home to him, there he is, running to meet us with arms open wide. What a wonderful image! We sometimes make the same mistakes over and over, yet each time we come to him with a repentant heart, he forgives us. His forgiveness never runs out.

Because God forgives us so completely, we should pass on his gracious attitude, fully forgiving those who wrong us. Instead, sometimes when we forgive, we hold back a little grudge—ammunition for a future argument. We may speak complete forgiveness and even feel a bit sacrificial because we forgave so generously. But inside, where only we (and God) can see, we haven't really forgotten that wrong. We've stored it on a mental shelf for future use against our friend or loved one.

Of course, if one of our friends plays this same game and brings up something that happened years ago, which we thought was ancient history, we are quick to shout, "Unfair! That thing is over and done with!" Yeah, right.

The challenge for today: From the prodigal's dad, learn to forgive and forget. Ask for God's help—he's an expert in this field. After all, we give him plenty of practice.

"If [he] sins against you seven times in a day, and seven times comes back to you and says, 'I repent,' forgive him." —LUKE 17:4

Keep On Asking

KNOCK! KNOCK! KNOCK! "GET UP, NEIGH-bor. Come on, answer your door!"

"Do you know what time it is?" The groggy man leaned out his window and loudly whispered. "Go away! You're going to wake up the entire neighborhood."

"Wait, don't go back to bed. I need your help. A friend from out of town stopped by late tonight, and I don't have any food. Can I borrow a loaf of bread?"

"Look, it's late. My kids are in bed . . . in fact, I was in bed before you woke me."

"I know. Please help me out. I'm sorry I had to wake you, but I'll be embarrassed in front of my out-of-town company if you don't help me. Come on, I have to serve him something."

"Go away!" the man pulled his head back inside the window.

Knock! Knock! Knock! "Please, help me. I would do it for you, and you know that."

"I said to go . . ." the man stopped and let out a loud sigh. "OK, I'll be down in a minute. Figure out exactly what you need."

BASED ON LUKE 11:5–8

139

Reflections From The Heart

"Can I . . . I want . . .Will you . . .?" How do you respond to per-sistent pestering? Grab the duct tape and close the offender's mouth? Tempting, eh? Some people don't respond well to being pestered. They tend to get a little impatient and stubborn. Eventually, they may give in just to shut the person up (that's what the kids usually hope for, isn't it?).

Jesus told this story to encourage us in our prayer lives. When you want God to do something, bring it to his attention, and don't be afraid to be specific. Tell him exactly what you need and how you feel about the situation. Whenever anything is weigh-ing on your heart, it is best to get it out in the open with him. As you are praying, be sensitive to God. He may desire to change your heart on the subject. Remember that he loves you and, just as you desire to give good gifts to those you love, he wants to give good things to you.

The challenge for today: Don't worry about pestering God. When something is on your heart, pray constantly about it.

"Pray continually." —1 Thessalonians 5:17

Arrogance Personified

THE CROWD PARTED LIKE THE RED SEA for the finely dressed Pharisee to pass through. He didn't make eye contact with anyone. In fact, he made every effort not to touch any of the people crowding the aisles of the temple. By the way he carried himself, it was apparent that he believed he was better than any other person there.

Gliding through the temple, he stopped in a crowded area. People moved away, forming a wide circle around him. "Look at his fine robe," said one. "I want to hear his prayers," said another. "He's such an important religious man. I'm sure he is very close to God, and his prayers will show it."

Everyone hushed as he began praying. "Ohhh God, I'm so thankful that I'm not like the sinners here in the temple today," he cried. "After all, I'm not a robber or adulterer. You are so fortunate to have me as your friend, God. I'm so much better than the others here—especially that tax collector over there." The people around the Pharisee were somewhat surprised at his arrogant, unrepentant prayers.

Meanwhile, the tax collector he referred to was entering the temple. The people parted for him, too, though not out of respect, as they had for the Pharisee. No one liked the tax collector, and no one wanted to be near him. The tax collector knelt with his head bowed to the floor. His heart was so humble that he couldn't even raise his eyes. "Oh God, have mercy on me. I'm a sinner and I need your forgiveness. I am so unworthy of your love, Father."

BASED ON LUKE 18:9–14

 ## Reflections From The Heart

"Hey God, you're soooo lucky that I'm on your side. I know you can do a lot more good in the world because I'm on your team. You probably wish you had thousands like me instead of those other losers."

What arrogance! This Pharisee thought he was so very valuable. He seemed to think he was even more important than God.

But before we judge him, lets ask ourselves if we've ever acted like a Christian snob. Do we sometimes look around and do a little spiritual comparing between ourselves and others? Perhaps we inwardly boast that our gifts exceed theirs or that at least we've conquered *that* sin. It is much the same as when women look around and think, *OK, her hips are bigger than mine*, or *I've got less chins than she does . . . I'm a better singer . . . she's more artistic . . . my kids are better students.*

Approaching God with this attitude will not get you very far. An unrepentant heart is closed to God. It doesn't believe what Scripture says—we are *all* sinners.

On the other hand, the tax collector recognized his need for God's mercy and forgiveness. Because he approached God humbly, his heart was pliable and teachable, and he showed respect and honor for God.

The challenge for today: Don't compare yourself to any other Christian, either to lift yourself up or to push her down. Come before God with a humble heart. Recognize your personal need for mercy and forgiveness.

"For whoever exalts himself will be humbled, and whoever humbles himself will be exalted." —MATTHEW 23:12

Use It or Lose It

"I'M GOING AWAY ON A LONG TRIP," THE wealthy master announced to his trusted servants. "I'm entrusting you three with my money. Remember, my money is important to me, so be careful with it." He clapped his hands and a servant brought a tray with eight velvet bags on it. Each bag bulged with gold coins. "Give five bags to the first man," the master said. He looked the servant in the eyes and said, "I'm trusting you." Then he turned to the second servant and ordered that two bags be given to him. The third servant was given one bag. The next day the master left, and no one knew when he would return.

After a very long time, the master came home. He immediately called the three servants in to give an account of his money. "Sir, I invested your five bags of gold and earned five more bags," the first servant said, presenting ten bags to his master.

"Excellent! You have shown that you were quite worthy of my trust," the master replied. "I will trust you with even more responsibility."

The second servant also had invested the gold given to him. "I doubled your money, too" he said, giving the master four bags of gold. The master was pleased with him and promised him more responsibility.

The third servant said, "I was afraid because I know how important your money is to you. I didn't want to take a chance of losing your bag of gold, so I buried it and kept it safe." He handed the muddy velvet bag to his master.

"You lazy man," the master exploded. "You didn't even put it in the bank to earn interest? Take his bag and give it to the first servant. Get this man out of my sight!"

Based on Matthew 25:14–30

 Reflections From The Heart

Maybe the stock market isn't your thing. Maybe investing in CDs and Roth IRAs just doesn't interest you (or maybe it does—you go, girl!). But look at this story of investing from the perspective of using the gifts and talents God has given you. Scripture says that God has given all believers gifts, and that it takes all of us working together to make the body of Christ effective (1 Corinthians 12).

Think about this: God didn't have to give us talents and gifts, just as the master didn't have to entrust his precious money to the servants. He chose to, and by doing so, he allows us to be involved in his work.

Just as the master trusted his three servants to do the right thing, God expects us to make the right choices regarding our gifts. He expects the best from us, but allows us to use our free will and our minds as we decide how to invest those gifts.

The third servant learned a tough lesson—use it or lose it. The bag of money that he didn't use was taken from him and given to one of the servants who made better choices.

What talents or gifts has God given you? Music, speaking, writing, teaching, generosity, hospitality? What are you good at and what do you enjoy? How are you using this gift for God's kingdom? What joys or blessings have you realized by serving and sharing your gift?

The challenge for today: Use it or lose it. If you haven't identified your gifts or talents, ask a close friend to tell you what she sees as your strengths. And ask God to confirm and help you use your gifts.

"The body is a unit, though it is made up of many parts; and though all its parts are many, they form one body."

—1 CORINTHIANS 12:12

Touch of Love

EVERYWHERE JESUS WENT, PEOPLE swarmed around him. His reputation quickly grew as the news of his healings spread across the countryside. When he passed through towns, people crowded the streets, dragging their sick, blind, or crippled friends and relatives to him. It was hard for Jesus to find time to eat or even sleep. He cared so much about people that he didn't want to turn anyone away. Some of the horribly deformed or seriously ill people who came before him turned the stomachs of his followers, but Jesus never batted an eye.

One particular day, Jesus and his friends were walking near the outskirts of a town when a voice called to him from a grove of trees. Jesus stopped and looked around, and a man hobbled toward him. "Leper!" someone shouted, as he grabbed Jesus to pull him away from the man. "Don't touch him—it's contagious. Very contagious!"

The man hung his head, but through the rags covering his misshapen face he whispered, "Lord, if you are willing, you can make me clean."

Jesus looked at the man. The deadly disease was eating away his body, but Jesus looked in his eyes. He saw the soul of a lonely man who was forbidden from being around people. This was a man who probably had not seen his family for years—a man who was simply waiting to die. A man who had faith to believe that Jesus could heal him. Jesus slowly raised his hand . . . and touched the leper's face. "I am willing," he said. "Be clean." Immediately the leprosy left the man. He was completely healed.

BASED ON LUKE 5:12–16

 ## Reflections From The Heart

Did you catch that—Jesus touched him! A man whom society shunned and people feared—a man with a highly contagious, socially unacceptable disease. We're not talking about a cold that might put you down for a while. We're talking about a disease that took you away from family and friends and eventually killed you, slowly and painfully.

Jesus, the almighty Son of God, an important man with a mission, risked contracting leprosy by touching this sick man. Jesus knew that the man probably had not felt a touch in years. He knew what statistics have proven to be true today, that touch, the feel of skin on skin, is vital to the human spirit. So, as Jesus healed the man's body, he also began healing his spirit. View it as a sort of welcome-back-to-the-human-race touch. Jesus could have healed him with a word or even a thought. But Jesus chose to touch him.

Are you willing to get down and dirty to help others? Or are you happy to support them with money or in prayer (both of which are important), but you would rather not get physically involved? Would you cuddle a baby who is HIV positive? Would you serve dinner to drug addicts or homeless people? Of course, it's important to share the gospel with people—it's the most important thing we can do. But what other practical ways can we help people, realizing that it's hard to listen or respond to any message when you're hungry or cold?

The challenge for today: Reach out and touch someone. Let the love of Jesus flow through you—skin to skin.

"Serve wholeheartedly, as if you were serving the Lord, not men."
—EPHESIANS 6:7

Gettin' Out
of the Boat

THE TWELVE TIRED MEN CLIMBED INTO the boat and began rowing across the lake. The only sounds were the swoosh of the oars dragging through the water and an occasional yawn from one of the men. But, as so often happened on this moody sea, a violent storm blew up from nowhere. The disciples knew they had a problem. "Peter, you're the strongest. You take my place on the oars," John shouted over the wind.

"I'll row, but, we're in serious trouble," Peter shouted back. The harder they rowed, the harder the wind blew. They weren't making any progress. Panic tugged at each man's heart, a single thought uniting them—*We need Jesus. He'd get us out of this mess.*

"Hey, what's that?" James pointed into the darkness. It was hard to see what he was pointing at through the pounding waves.

"I see it. It looks like a ghost!" someone shouted. They forgot all about rowing, straining to see through the storm. Fear gripped their hearts, and they were too tired to fight it. It had been such a long day.

"Don't be afraid. It's me," the ghostlike figure called. Slowly, it dawned on Peter that the voice belonged to Jesus. Jesus was walking on top of the water—through a raging storm!

"Master, if it's really you, let me come to you . . . on top of the water," Peter cried. When Jesus said, "Come on," Peter was out of the boat in an instant. His feet barely touched the top of the water as he loped toward Jesus, his eyes glued on his friend's face. But, when a big wave slapped him in the face, Peter suddenly realized that he was . . . walking on water! He looked back at the other guys in the boat, then around at the splashing waves, and promptly began to sink into the angry sea. "Help me!" he managed to scream before going under water.

Instantly, Jesus was at his side, lifting Peter out of the water and helping him into the boat. Jesus sighed, "Peter, your faith is so small."

As the other disciples watched this happen, each man dropped to his knees. "You really are the Son of God," they whispered in awe.

BASED ON MATTHEW 14:22–33

 Reflections From The Heart

Don't you love this story? Peter may have been impulsive; he may have been emotional, but he had some experiences that the staid, calm, stay-in-the-boat disciples didn't have. His faith was enthusiastic and real. When Jesus said, "Come!" Peter was out of that boat in a New York minute. He was willing to try pretty much whatever Jesus said.

How often do I miss the blessings of an exciting relationship with God because I am . . . chicken? It's easy and safe to stay in the boat, smacking my oars against the same old waves and sometimes even rowing in circles. The problem is, nothing ever changes. Day in and day out, my relationship with God stays pretty much the same. I become a status quo Christian. My own perceived limitations and my fears keep me from giving God a chance to show me new and exciting things, or to use me in ways that go beyond my wildest dreams.

The challenge for today: *Get out of the boat!* Lock your eyes on Jesus and step onto the water. If you must, just take one baby step at a time out of your comfort zone. Let God show you new and exciting things about life with him. Give him a chance to use you in ways you never dreamed were possible. Don't look back at the guys you left in the boat; keep your eyes on Jesus, and be prepared for him to do magnificent, exciting works through you. Don't be afraid to get wet; don't even be afraid to sink a little bit. Trust him to be at your side instantly, lifting you up and brushing your wet hair out of your eyes. Remember that he's out there on the water, in the middle of a raging storm. He can handle it, and he will help you handle it, too.

"If you have faith and do not doubt, not only can you do what was done to the fig tree, but also you can say to this mountain, 'Go, throw yourself into the sea,' and it will be done." —MATTHEW 21:21

Saying What You Mean

LAZARUS WAS SICK AND, NO MATTER what his sisters tried, he kept getting worse. "Martha, let's send for Jesus. He isn't far away and I know he can help."

Mary and Martha sent a message to Jesus, telling him that his friend was very ill. Then they waited for him to come. "Where is he? Why hasn't Jesus come?" Mary's voice was filled with hurt. "We sent for him two days ago, and Lazarus keeps getting worse."

"I know. I thought Jesus would be here by now, too." Martha was angry. "If he doesn't come soon, Lazarus will die."

Martha's words were prophetic. That very day her brother died . . . and still Jesus didn't come. As the sisters carried out the funeral preparations, a feeling of betrayal settled over them. Jesus was a good friend who had stayed in their home and enjoyed their hospitality many times. This time they desperately needed him, and he didn't come.

A few days after the funeral, the sisters heard someone shouting, "Jesus is coming!"

Mary and Martha looked at each other in disbelief. "Now he comes? Where was he when we needed him?" Martha didn't even try to control her anger. She marched right up to Jesus and said, "It's too late; Lazarus is dead. He would still be alive if you had come when we sent for you."

"Take me to the tomb." Jesus could barely get the words out, and his eyes filled with tears. They led him to the cave where Lazarus was buried. "Move the stone," Jesus ordered.

"No," someone cautioned, "he's been dead four days—the smell will be awful!" But, Jesus wasn't negotiating. He waved to the men, and they rolled the huge stone away from the opening.

Jesus slowly raised his eyes to the sky and said, "Father, thank you for hearing my prayer." Then he took a deep breath and shouted. "Lazarus, come out!"

Mary buried her face on Martha's shoulder, but Martha kept her eyes on the cave door. She didn't even dare take a breath. When Martha's knees buckled, Mary looked up. Lazarus was standing in the door of the tomb—alive.

BASED ON JOHN 11:1–44

 ## Reflections From The Heart

Don't you love Martha? She seems to have always let people know where they stood. She didn't pull any punches, and she said what was on her mind. After Lazarus's death, Martha was hurting, and she told Jesus exactly how she felt. She didn't spout any Christian jargon or holy words. She said exactly what was in her heart. And why not? Jesus knew what she was thinking anyway. He saw her pain and disappointment, and he could handle it when she said it out loud. He listened, then he answered by showing her why her faith should remain strong.

When you pray, do you feel the need to say what is *expected?* Have you been taught that Christians never show disappointment or fear? Or that we are never to voice our lack of faith or (God forbid) anger? Do you fill your prayers with the right words—the Christian words—instead of what is truly in your heart?

Who do you think you're fooling? How shallow is your God? Remember, he looks at the heart. He knows what you're feeling, and he can take it if you verbalize it to him. Your fancy prayers may impress other people with how well you're dealing with difficulties, but you're not fooling God.

The challenge for today: Be honest with God. He can handle it. Realize that the sooner you are honest with him, the sooner you can move forward and grow to new depths in your faith.

"The LORD does not look at the things man looks at. Man looks at the outward appearance, but the LORD looks at the heart."

—1 SAMUEL 16:7

Never Give Up

A SHEPHERD STOOD IN A FIELD OF GREEN grass counting his sheep as they settled in for the night. "Ninety seven, ninety eight, ninety nine . . . ninety nine? Where's my last sheep?" The shepherd looked all around as darkness settled. After he made sure that the ninety-nine sheep were safe from wild animals, he left them to look for the missing sheep. The shepherd backtracked the route the flock had traveled that day. He looked in valleys and gullies, searching anywhere the little sheep could have gotten lost. The night sky grew dark, and still the shepherd searched, thankful for the bright moonlight and stars.

Finally, he saw the white fleece of the little sheep huddled behind a rock. It looked forlorn and frightened. The tired shepherd climbed over rocks and gently petted the little animal, putting it at ease with his gentle touch and soft, soothing words. It looked at him with what appeared to be relief and gratefulness. The shepherd then lifted the sheep to his shoulders and hiked back to the rest of the flock. "Hey, you critters, celebrate with me!

Our family is complete once again!" Then he called to his friends and neighbors, "Join the party! I've found my lost sheep."

BASED ON LUKE 15:1–7

 Reflections From The Heart

Now, where is the wisdom in a shepherd leaving his ninety-nine sheep to go look for one lost lamb? Wouldn't you think he would just write off that lost one and take care of the big group that had stuck with him and been obedient? He took a chance by leaving the flock alone; predators could have attacked them, or some of them could have wandered away while he was searching for the lost sheep.

Jesus told this story to show us the depths of God's love. God doesn't close the gates to his family by saying, "Well, I have this many believers now, so I'm not going to worry about that one over there who hasn't yet decided to follow me. I don't really need him." God doesn't work that way. He wants everyone to have the chance to be a part of his family. When a person decides to accept Jesus Christ as his or her Savior, it is party time in heaven! Even the angels celebrate.

Because we don't know who eventually will accept Christ and who won't, we should continually be open to sharing the message of God's love. The shepherd is seeking those with whom we come in contact and he may use us to help bring them home to his flock.

The challenge for today: Don't be passive. Share the plan of salvation with those who don't know Christ. Remember it's not your responsibility to decide who should hear and who is hope-less. That's God's call.

"How great is the love the Father has lavished on us, that we should be called children of God!" —1 JOHN 3:1

A Servant's Heart

JESUS KNEW THAT VERY SOON HIS PUR-
pose for coming to earth would be fulfilled. It
was time to make a bold statement to his followers.
That night, his twelve disciples gathered for dinner.
As they enjoyed the food and talked among themselves, Jesus quietly took off his robe and tied a towel around his waist. Picking
up a bowl of water, he went to his friend seated at the end of the
table, knelt down, and began to wash that man's feet. Hands
halted in midair and conversation stopped abruptly as the twelve
men realized that their leader was performing a lowly chore—
something a servant would do.

In the astonished silence that blanketed the room, Jesus
moved around the table, washing and drying each man's feet.
When he came to Peter, the big fisherman pulled his feet under
his robe and said, "No, you will not wash my feet!"

Jesus looked deep into Peter's eyes. "If I don't wash your feet,
you have no part of me," he said quietly.

Peter slid his feet into Jesus' hands. "Then wash them. In fact,
wash my whole body!"

Jesus explained that Peter's body was already clean; only his feet needed washing. Then Jesus finished washing everyone's feet. Finally he stood up and put his robe back on. "I have done this as an example to you. Each of you should serve others as I have served you. If you know my father's love, serve one another."

BASED ON JOHN 13:1–17

 ## Reflections From The Heart

Jesus knew that his time on earth was coming to a close. He had spent three years teaching his disciples how to live and love for God. Then he took an opportunity to pound home his message once more. It was time to cut through all the squabbles about who or what was important, and to learn to serve others.

Jesus taught this lesson by example. In love, he voluntarily took the lowest spot and did the work of a slave, washing his disciples' feet. Jesus wanted these men to understand that a servant bows lower than the one being served. All pretense of importance goes out the window as the servant picks up a dirty foot and washes away the mud and dust of the day.

Peter tried to stop him, but Jesus pointed out that Peter would have no future with him if he didn't let Jesus wash his feet. Interesting, isn't it? It takes two to serve—one to do the serving and one to be served.

Do you have a servant's heart? Are you willing to show love and compassion for others by doing things for them? Are you willing to humble yourself by doing work that is not glamorous or desirable? Think about how you connect with other people as you serve, and what image you portray of God's love.

The challenge for today: Take a cue from a Jewish carpenter who is the Savior of all mankind. Take off your coat, get down on your knees, and humbly serve.

"This is how we know what love is: Jesus Christ laid down his life for us. And we ought to lay down our lives for our brothers."
—1 JOHN 3:16

Celebrate!

Jesus' friends hid their eyes. Some turned away, and others left. It was hard to watch what was happening to him. The Roman soldiers beat him, nailed him to a wooden cross, and laughed when he died. No one tried to stop them—the whole thing had been sur- real. They had arrested him in the middle of the night, and the kangaroo court pushed through a sentence before the sun came up. He was hanging on the cross before some people even knew what had happened.

When they pulled Jesus' body down and carried it to the tomb, life seemed to drain from most of his followers. They believed in him—believed he was the Messiah. Now he was dead. The church leaders themselves were the ones who pushed through his murder. Why didn't God stop it?

As soon as the Sabbath was over, three women dragged them- selves to the tomb carrying spices and perfumes. Even though they had lost hope, they made themselves follow tradition and properly anoint his body. It was the last gift they could give him. Approaching the tomb, they wondered aloud how they would be able to move the large stone that covered the doorway. It had taken several strong soldiers to roll it into place. They felt overwhelmed as they considered this task—so much had happened in the last week. This was too much to think about.

Rounding the last bend in the road, the first woman glanced up at the tomb. "It's gone! The stone is gone!" she cried. "Do you think they've stolen his body?" Confusion filled their hearts. They approached the tomb, cautiously going in. It was empty! Two men in shining white clothing suddenly stood beside them. The women dropped to the ground, shaking with fear.

"Why are you looking for the living in a place for the dead? He isn't here. He has risen, just as he told you he would!" the angels announced.

"He's alive!" the women sang, hugging and dancing for joy!

BASED ON LUKE 22:47–24:12

 ## Reflections From The Heart

These three women must have felt like their hearts were on yo-yo strings. One minute they are so sad they can barely function. A minute later, exuberance is bursting from their lips! Perhaps they had never really understood what Jesus meant when he talked about coming back to life. Or perhaps their faith was too small to believe it. We can forgive their depression; the events of the past few days must have been horrendous. If you've ever suffered along with someone who was dying, you know how draining it can be. It makes the women's joy at the news of the resurrection even more amazing.

The resurrection is the reason our faith is real. No other deity in any other religion has come back to life. Jesus Christ came to earth as a human, he taught, he healed, and he did other miracles. He was crucified, even though he had never done anything wrong. Three days later, he was alive again and is now back in heaven with his father. He endured all of this because he loves us and wanted to make a way for sinful people to live in heaven with God for eternity.

Jesus was the sacrifice for our sins—yours and mine. Every time we take that sacrifice lightly and act in selfishness or disobedience, we pound the nails into that cross once again. Rather, we should take seriously the reality of the crucifixion. It's basic to our faith. Do we understand why the women at the tomb on that first Easter morning celebrated? He's alive! And that makes all the difference.

The challenge for today: Celebrate! You don't have to wait until Easter to celebrate the resurrection. Thank God for the incredible gift of Jesus, and for the truth that even though he was killed, he didn't stay dead. He's alive!

"This is how God showed his love among us: He sent his one and only son into the world that we might live through him."

—1 JOHN 4:9

Seeing Beyond the Moment

A S THE TWO MEN WALKED DOWN THE road toward Emmaus, they talked about the horrible events of the past week—Jesus' arrest, laughable trial, and cruel crucifixion. The whole thing was railroaded through, like someone couldn't wait to see him dead.

"The whole thing seems so unreal. I feel like I've been walking around in a nightmare for the past few days. Did you see how they treated him? And he didn't say a word. Were you still around when they buried him?" Cleopas asked.

"No, I left during the crucifixion. I know I should have stayed, but I just couldn't take it. The Romans were so mean. I thought Jesus was the answer to all our problems. I can't believe he's dead. What about his teachings? Maybe they weren't even true. I don't know what I believe anymore."

"Hello friends, may I walk along with you?" They hadn't heard the stranger approach. He listened to them talk for a while, then asked, "What's the problem?"

"Are you the only man in Jerusalem who doesn't know about the things that have happened here?"

"What things?" he asked.

The pain in their hearts spilled out as they told him about Jesus of Nazareth, who healed the sick, raised the dead, and taught about God. They spared no details of how the chief priests had him arrested, pushed through a trial, and then crucified him. "Then today, some of our women went to his tomb, and his body is missing!"

The stranger started discussing the Scriptures, beginning back with Moses, and explaining what they said about the Messiah. When they neared Emmaus, the two men invited the stranger to join them for dinner. They wanted to hear what else he might say.

After sitting down at the table, their guest took the bread and blessed it. Then he broke it apart and handed some to each of them. At that very moment, they realized that the stranger was Jesus! Immediately, he disappeared from the room.

BASED ON LUKE 24:13–35

 Reflections From The Heart

Why didn't the men on the road to Emmaus recognize Jesus? He was the very man they were mourning—the one they couldn't stop talking about. Yet, when he walked up beside them, they didn't seem to have any idea who he was.

Have you ever been so upset and confused that you couldn't see anything past the pain in your heart? Did it consume you so that it colored everything else in the world? You may have been so far down that you had to look up to see rock bottom.

We might be able to excuse these two men for not recognizing the Savior—their pain was so fresh. But, this is something we need to be careful about. We shouldn't get so wrapped up in our pain that we miss seeing the Savior. Once we have received Christ as Savior, we are never, ever alone. That's sometimes hard to remember in the dark places of life, but that's when it's most important to remember. Knowing that he is with us can help us through those hard times. He hasn't promised us a bed of roses, but he did promise that whatever comes, we won't go through the hard times alone.

The challenge for today: In the midst of your pain and distress, keep the door of your heart open a crack, so you can see the Savior. Hold on to his presence for strength to get through the pain.

"Even though I walk through the valley of the shadow of death, I will fear no evil, for you are with me; your rod and your staff, they comfort me." —PSALM 23:4

"Show Me"

THOMAS PUSHED PETER AWAY AND stomped across the room. "I don't believe you! Stop saying that Jesus is alive. I saw him die. It's over, and the sooner you admit that, the sooner you can get on with life." Thomas shouted louder with each declaration.

"Shh." Peter was afraid Thomas's shouts would draw the attention of the Roman soldiers outside. "Just listen a minute. I know he died; don't forget, we were there, too. But, I'm telling you that we were all in this room the other day, with the door locked, and all of a sudden he was here. Jesus was here. He talked to us and showed us the wounds in his hands. It's true, Thomas!"

"I won't believe it unless I see him for myself . . . unless I touch the nail scars in his hands and the wounds in his side." Thomas left, slamming the door behind him.

About a week later, Thomas and the other disciples were together again in that very same locked room. Some were dozing, some were praying, Thomas was gazing out a window. Then a gentle voice broke into his thoughts. "Peace to you all." Thomas's eyes darted back into the room . . . and directly into Jesus' face. "Touch my hands and side, Thomas. Stop doubting and believe."

Thomas could barely speak. "My Lord and God," he finally whispered.

"You believe because you have seen me," Jesus said. "How blessed are those who have not seen me, but still believe."

BASED ON JOHN 20:24–29

 ## Reflections From The Heart

I'm from Missouri—the Show Me state. I wonder if Thomas was, too. For whatever reason, Thomas wasn't taking anybody's word regarding Jesus' resurrection. He was going to have to see it for himself before he would believe. Jesus pointed out to Thomas that it doesn't take much faith to believe what you can see and touch. He was more impressed with people who believe simply by faith, without any physical evidence of his resurrection.

Where does your faith fall on the Thomas scale? Do you need to see things, touch them, and smell them before you allow yourself to believe? Do you score pretty low? The Christian walk is based on faith—if you don't trust him enough to believe what he says, then you need to make some changes in your attitude and relationship with God.

The challenge for today: Walk by faith, live by faith, grow in faith. How do you do that? Pray, read his word, seek him, and take time to remember what he has done in the past.

"Though you have not seen him, you love him; and even though you do not see him now, you believe in him and are filled with an inexpressible and glorious joy, for you are receiving the goal of your faith, the salvation of your souls." —1 PETER 1:8–9

A Generous Friend

HEARTBROKEN SOBS FILLED THE TOWN of Joppa as news of Dorcas's death spread. "What are we going to do without her? She was the kindest, most generous woman I've ever known."

Dorcas had always pooh-poohed the praise for her generous gifts to the widows around town. "The only thing I can do is sew," she had always said. "I'm not a great cook or teacher. I can't sing, but I can sew. So, I'm happy to make clothing and give it to those less fortunate than I am. The joy in a woman's face when she gets a new dress or coat is worth every stitch!" Those widows she had so kindly helped would miss Dorcas as much as her own family. She had been a true example of God's love.

"Peter is in a nearby town. God has helped him do miracles before, maybe he could help," one woman said. Some thought she was grasping at straws; others believed it was worth a try.

Peter came right away and his heart was moved by the tearful stories of Dorcas's generosity. He sent everyone out of the room and knelt by her body. "Get up," he gently ordered. She opened her eyes and sat up. Peter called Dorcas's friends back into the room and presented her to them—alive and well. Joy filled Joppa that day!

BASED ON ACTS 9:36-42

 Reflections From The Heart

Dorcas had endeared herself to people because of her generous spirit. She used her talent (sewing) to make gifts for people who probably didn't often get new things. These women had no way to repay Dorcas, except with a warm hug and a smile. When Dorcas died, she left a big hole in her friends' lives, so they did something about it. They cried out to God through Peter and he heard their prayers. Clearly, Dorcas meant a lot to her friends.

Do you have a friend who means very much to you? If so, you are very fortunate. In our busy world, good friends aren't as easy to come by as they once were. Tell her how important she is to you.

Are you generous toward others as Dorcas was? Do you find ways to share? Do you take time to actually do things for others—not just send money to a cause but use your physical gifts and talents to do something nice for someone else? You could cook a meal, drive to the grocery store, defrost a freezer, cut the grass, send an encouraging card, or find other ways to meet needs. It feels good to help someone . . . especially someone who doesn't have the health or the means to repay you.

The challenge for today: Look for ways to encourage others and to help them grow deeper in their relationship with Christ.

"Let us consider how we may spur one another on toward love and good deeds." —HEBREWS 10:24

Going Outside the Lines

PETER WAS KNOWN TO BREAK A FEW rules in his time. Of all the disciples, he was the one who sometimes tested the boundaries or at least took a chance now and then. But the dream he just had was extreme, even for Peter.

In this mysterious dream, a sheet dropped down from the sky, right in front of Peter. One corner of it fell open and out rolled all sorts of animals, reptiles, and birds. Then he heard a voice say, "Kill these animals and eat them."

"No, I can't," Peter answered. "I've done a lot of crazy things in my time, but I won't eat animals that are forbidden by Jewish law!"

"If God says something is acceptable, don't argue," the voice said.

Peter had this same dream three times. "I don't know what it means," he told a friend, "and it's making me crazy!"

The previous day a few towns away, a Roman army officer named Cornelius had a weird dream of his own. He had fallen into a trance and had seen an angel coming toward him, calling his name.

"What is it, sir?" Cornelius answered.

"God has seen your kind heart, your gifts to the poor, and your prayers. He wants you to send for Peter. Ask him to come and teach you more about God."

Cornelius woke up, called his servants, and instructed them to fetch Peter.

When Cornelius's servants arrived at the house where Peter was staying and asked him to come teach at the home of a Roman army officer, Peter suddenly knew what his dream had meant. Before the dream, he would have said that it was unacceptable for a Jewish man to teach in the home of a Gentile, especially a Roman army officer. But through the dream, God had shown him that whatever the Lord says is acceptable . . . is acceptable.

BASED ON ACTS 10

Reflections From The Heart

Peter often stretched the limits of life, but being told in a dream that it was OK to eat forbidden foods seemed ridiculous. There were some things that even Peter wouldn't do. After God told him it was OK to do what the dream said, Peter still must have wondered. Finally, when Cornelius explained his own dream, it all made sense. But that doesn't mean it was easy for Peter.

What does the story of Peter and Cornelius say to you today? Jesus didn't come to earth just to save white middle-class Americans, or inner city Hispanics, or black women. No one group has a corner on Jesus' love. Of course, you know that, and you aren't opposed to the message of God's love being shared around the world with people from all walks of life . . . just as long as no one asks you to do it. Ouch! Are you settled in and comfy in your middle-class white suburb or black urban neighborhood, or wherever you call home? Probably not too far from you are homeless people waiting outside an understaffed food pantry, or shelters full of abused women and children who just need someone to talk to. Reaching out to those who aren't like you doesn't have to mean preaching a sermon or handing out tracts.

The challenge for today: Put feet on your faith and show God's love in practical ways—God's love with skin on it. You might have to go outside your comfort zone and learn how to relate to people with whom you don't have a lot in common. God can call you to reach out to anyone, so be open to his leading.

"You will be my witnesses in Jerusalem, and in all Judea and Samaria, and to the ends of the earth." —Acts 1:8

A Complete Turnaround

SAUL WAS A NASTY GUY—ARROGANT, opinionated, and not much fun to be around. His singular purpose in life was to make Christians as miserable as possible. He spent his days persecuting them and throwing some in jail, just because they were Christians. When he felt that his hometown was sufficiently cleared of the Christians, he headed for Damascus to clean up that town, too.

Traveling with a group of friends, conversation got heated as Saul spouted his angry views against Christians. In the middle of Saul's tirade, a brilliant light blasted from the sky directly on him. Blinded by the brilliance, Saul fell to his knees.

"Saul, why are you persecuting me?" asked a loud voice.

"Who are you?" Saul responded

"I am Jesus, the one you are persecuting," the voice answered.

Saul was quiet. This meant that the Christians were right . . . Jesus was real.

"Get up," the voice continued. "Go into the city and you will be told what to do."

Saul's friends stood around with their mouths hanging open. They heard the voice, but couldn't find where it came from. Saul tried to stand, but he needed help. He opened his eyes, but couldn't see anything. He was blind!

Saul obeyed everything Jesus told him to do. When his sight was given back to him, God changed his name to Paul . . . and everything about Paul's life was new. He turned away from the anger and persecution he had heaped on Christians. Now Paul devoted his life to teaching about Jesus, encouraging others to know him.

BASED ON ACTS 9

 Reflections From The Heart

Some people think that folks either hated Paul or loved him. It's doubtful that many people were on the fence where he was concerned. He was a powerfully focused man who gave his all to whatever he was doing. He wanted to get rid of Christians and stop the talk about Jesus, so he went after Christians with a vengeance.

On that road to Damascus, when he discovered that he had been wrong—Christ truly was the Son of God—he held nothing back from his newfound faith. He put that same energy into preaching and teaching about Christ and he was just as uncompromising as before, only on God's side this time.

Did you have a dramatic conversion, such as Paul did? Did you make a U-turn and leave your old life behind, as far behind as Paul did? Paul's story is a good reminder that you can't hold anything back when you become a Christian. It doesn't work to be a Christian on Sunday but live your old life the rest of the week. You can't have one foot in both worlds.

The challenge for today: Give the Christian life your all. Follow Paul's example and live for Christ with enthusiasm and conviction. Make a difference in the world around you . . . for God.

"Go and make disciples of all the nations, baptizing them in the name of the Father and of the Son and of the Holy Spirit."

—MATTHEW 28:19

Staying True in
Hard Times

PAUL AND SILAS'S FEET WERE LOCKED IN stocks deep in the center of the jail in Philippi. Mice and bugs crawled over their legs. Even so, they prayed out loud and sang joyful praises to God.

"Why don't you guys just shut up? In case you haven't noticed, you are in jail . . . God doesn't seem to be answering your prayers," growled one of the other prisoners.

"Aah, leave 'em alone. Kind of makes me feel better," said another voice in the darkness.

Around midnight Paul and Silas were still singing quietly when the floor began to shake and the stocks holding their feet fell apart. Silas was thrown into Paul's arms as walls shook and doors fell off their hinges.

"Earthquake!" someone shouted. Another prisoner yelled, "The door's open! Run!"

"Wait!" Paul called out. When the jailer came to check on his prisoners, he found that Paul and Silas had kept every prisoner inside the jail. He was so impressed that he asked them how he could come to know the God they sang about. Paul told the jailer and his whole family about God.

BASED ON ACTS 16:16–34

 ## Reflections From The Heart

When the rubber meets the road, what kinds of tread marks does your faith make? Paul was certainly known for his "talk." Scripture records his teachings and sermons. But he also walked the talk, as we see in this story. It wouldn't have been right for the prisoners to run away. And if they had, the jailer would have killed himself or been killed for allowing the prisoners to escape. By keeping them in the broken-down jail, Paul showed the reality of the God to whom he had been singing.

No doubt you can "talk the talk" of the Christian life, at least to some extent. You can say the right words regarding God's love and concern for the world, living an honest life, honoring God, and so on. But how are you at living what you talk, in the easy times and when the going gets tough? Does your life look different from your non-Christian friends? Is your community affected by your presence? If you're no different from anyone else, why would anyone want your faith?

The challenge for today: Remember, your attitude shows. It seeps out when you least expect it. So if you're going to talk the Christian life, be careful to also walk it.

"You are the salt of the earth . . . You are the light of the world . . . let your light shine before men, that they may see your good deeds and praise your Father in heaven." —MATTHEW 5:13–14, 16